UnCorinthian Leadership

UnCorinthian Leadership

Thematic Reflections on 1 Corinthians

DAVID I. STARLING

Foreword by
CARL TRUEMAN

CASCADE *Books* · Eugene, Oregon

Cascade Books
An Imprint of Wipf and Stock Publishers
199 W. 8th Ave., Suite 3
Eugene, OR 97401

www.wipfandstock.com

ISBN 13: 978-1-62032-792-0

Cataloging-in-Publication data:

Starling, David I.

    UnCorinthian leadership : thematic reflections on 1 Corinthians / David I. Starling.

    xiv + 114 p. ; 23 cm. —Includes bibliographical references.

    ISBN 13: 978-1-62032-792-0

    1. Bible. Corinthians, 1st—Criticism, interpretation, etc. 2. Leadership—Biblical teaching. I. Title.

BS2675.6 L42 S83 2014

Manufactured in the U.S.A.

For Brian Powell
1 Cor 16:18b

Table of Contents

Foreword

THROUGHOUT HISTORY, THE CHURCH has often opposed the values and customs of the culture of the wider world not so much by rejecting them as by competing with them. Thus, in the fourth century, Athanasius wrote a life of the holy man, Anthony, in which Anthony was portrayed as being able to pursue the pagan ascetic ideal yet at a much higher level than the representatives of the pagan culture. In the high Middle Ages, the church was barely distinguishable from the secular authorities in the way it prosecuted its business, even to the point of pursuing military campaigns. Calvin, the hero of Reformed Protestants everywhere, was not averse to using the civil magistrate to expedite business when he felt it was necessary. And in our own day we are all familiar with the embarrassing spectacle of church leaders flaunting the health and vibrancy of their sex lives as a way of showing that the gospel allows one to have the values of the pagans only in a much more impressive form. Yet the Bible itself never presents Christianity as the perfection of worldly notions of virtue. It presents Christianity as an alternative to such and, indeed, as something that often stands as a judgment against the way the world turns.

In the current climate, this problem is nowhere more apparent than in approaches to church leadership. Celebrity culture, focused as it is on the charismatic individual, pervades the American evangelical landscape and, as recent years have shown, the conservative, reformed wings of this type of Christianity are saturated in such. Further, the combination of management theory and the emergence of the celebrity CEO in the wider world have also shaped evangelical notions of leadership. It is not only the hipster-chic skinny jean pastors who ape the world; it can also be the sharp-suited, straight-talking strong man.

Of course, there are things that Christian leaders can learn from the world's culture of leadership. Basic people skills, team building, and resolving conflicts are all areas where we can draw helpful lessons from the secular world. I remember when I took on my role as a seminary Vice President, I read a book or two on the leadership approach of Ernest Shackleton, the great polar explorer. His gift at assessing people's strengths and weaknesses, and at knowing who should do what task and with whom, was exceptional and gave me some insights I was able to employ in the seminary (a considerably less harsh environment than the South Pole, I hasten to add). Some aspects of leadership are purely technical and the world can teach us much in that regard.

Yet at root, the Christian notion of what a leader is to be is determined by Scripture, not by worldly criteria. The church leader does not represent the idealized and perfected worldly leader. Nor can the Christian take an abstract concept of leadership and simply fill it with Christian content. For the Christian, the very definition of what leadership is needs to be drawn from Scripture. Form and content are both to be biblical and to be perfectly matched.

The Bible contains many passages that speak to this issue but perhaps the most fertile book on the subject is 1 Corinthians. In fact, this book is not only the most fertile soil for thinking about Christian leadership, it is also the most timely. Paul writes about true Christian leadership to a church torn apart by the cult of celebrity and by sexual immorality—in other words, a church that drew its notions of leaders and leadership from the surrounding culture and that also reflected the morality of the same. We too live at a time when the wider culture, in terms of celebrity and sexual obsession, has penetrated the church. To read Paul to the Corinthians is truly to look in a mirror and see our present age.

For this reason, it is a great pleasure to have been invited to write the foreword of David Starling's new book. I have only met David once, and that very briefly, but it is clear from this volume that we share common concerns about current trends in Christian leadership, about the need for a biblically-based response, and about our own personal weaknesses and failings as we seek to fulfill leadership roles in our own spheres. This is not a commentary on 1 Corinthians, though David is a careful exegete and commentator; rather it is a cumulative series of reflections on the lessons of 1 Corinthians for the church in these last days. It is a welcome addition to the literature, a helpful corrective to the all-too-common rubbish written on the theme, and an encouraging challenge to us all to be conformed more closely to the mind of Christ, not simply in our personal lives but, most important of all, in our corporate church lives. I hope it is widely read. It deserves to be so.

Carl R. Trueman
Paul Woolley Professor of Church History,
Westminster Theological Seminary, PA
Pastor, Cornerstone Presbyterian Church, Ambler, PA

Preface

THIS BOOK HAD ITS origins in an invitation to speak at the annual "leader-ship summit" of the Sydney University Evangelical Union in February 2012. The invitation aroused mixed feelings: on the one hand, a sense of privilege and pleasure at the prospect of catching up with old friends and the chance to contribute something to a group that had played such a crucial role in my own discipleship; on the other hand, a certain discomfort with the way in which the notion of "leadership" is singled out for such focus among Christians in our day, and a degree of uncertainty about whether my own way of approaching the topic would fit the bill for a conference (let alone a "summit"!) devoted to it.

I talked over my tangled mix of enthusiasms and misgivings with the organizers of the conference and they graciously persevered in extending the invitation. So I accepted, and the conference turned out to be a delight-fully stimulating and encouraging occasion, full of rich conversations and sharp, searching questions. I am glad to have the opportunity to express my gratitude to Haydn Oakes, Rowan Kemp, and the whole team responsible for the conference, along with the many members and staff-workers of the EU, past and present, who have been a blessing to me in countless ways over the years.

The process of turning the conference talks into a book generated a whole new set of debts of gratitude. Christian Amondson, Chris Spinks, and the team at Cascade Books took the risk of commissioning a book by an unknown Australian, and offered expert assistance along the way. Ross Clifford, my principal at Morling College, granted me a semester of study leave in the first half of 2013, some of which was spent on this project; the Morling Foundation, the Australian College of Theology and the MCD

University of Divinity also contributed to some of the costs incurred during that semester. Tyndale House in Cambridge was a wonderful environment in which to work on the project, and I am thankful to the many friends and colleagues with whom I was able to talk over the ideas of the book while I was there. The chance to work through some of the contents of the book in seminar form at the Porterbrook Seminary in Sheffield was also a welcome opportunity, and stimulated further thought on the implications of 1 Corinthians for our contemporary social context. The whole semester spent in the UK would not have been possible without the loving enthusiasm and the creative and energetic labors of my wife Nicole—in this project, as in all things, she has been my closest companion and partner in the service of the Lord Jesus.

A wide circle of friends and colleagues generously gave of their time and expertise in reading the manuscript and offering comments and suggestions: particular thanks go to Don Carson, Andrew Clarke, Jon Coody, Duane Litfin, Brian Rosner, and Carl Trueman (who kindly agreed to write the foreword). Standing behind the book too is the privileged opportunity I have had over the years to spend time thinking through 1 Corinthians with students and fellow-lecturers at Morling College. It has been a delight to share my 1 Corinthians classes with colleagues as dedicated and accomplished as Brian Powell and, more recently, Tim MacBride. The publication of this book gives me an opportunity to put on record my deep sense of gratitude to Brian, who has been to me in various overlapping seasons a teacher, a colleague, a mentor, and a friend. In all of those roles I have been blessed by his integrity, humility, generosity and wisdom, so I am glad to have the chance to express my appreciation and to wish him (belatedly) a joyful and fruitful retirement.

one

INTRODUCTION

The man next to you on the London-to-Edinburgh train going north, wired up to his laptop and his mobile simultaneously: issuing instructions about hiring, firing, sidelining, expanding here and reducing here, letting so and so in on the latest developments, leaving so and so out of them, making cautious inquiries concerning new development opportunities, closing down an unprofitable field before it sinks too many resources.

Yes, he may well be a systems manager for an information technology firm. Or, he may equally well be a Baptist minister.[1]

The Word that Launched a Thousand Books

Anyone writing a new book about Christian leadership had better have a pretty good excuse. There is already, after all, a never-failing stream of similar publications pouring from the presses and flooding onto the shelves of Christian bookshops. Do we really need another?

In the world of contemporary Western Christianity, it seems, everyone loves "leadership." It's a word that crops up again and again in the language of Christian schools and university groups and conferences and seminaries—we all believe in leadership, we talk at great length about the importance of identifying and training leaders, and it is commonly the first

1. Milbank, "Stale Expressions," 264.

word we reach for in our mission statements and our marketing publications to describe what it is that we exist to foster and to develop.

This leadership-fixation of contemporary Western Christians corresponds to a similar phenomenon in the secular culture of our day. Harvard professor Barbara Kellerman paints a dizzying picture of the ever-growing immensity of what she calls the "leadership industry"—"my catchall term for the now countless leadership centers, institutes, programs, courses, seminars, workshops, experiences, trainers, books, blogs, articles, websites, webinars, videos, conferences, consultants, and coaches claiming to teach people—usually for money—how to lead." She comments: "Being a leader has become a mantra. It is a presumed path to money and power; a medium for achievement, both individual and institutional; and a mechanism for creating change sometimes—though hardly always—for the common good."[2]

It is no coincidence, as Kellerman notes, that the words "leader" and "leadership" have found their way into the mission statements of almost every single one of Harvard's professional schools, including the law school, the medical school, the divinity school, and the school of education.[3] In the publishing marketplace, too, the "leadership industry" has had an enormous impact: "In the early 1980s an average of three books on leadership were published each year; by the end of the decade that number was twenty-three. By now, of course, the number of leadership books (and other related materials) is somewhere in the stratosphere (a Google search of leadership books returns more than 84 million results)."[4]

The output of the Christian publishing industry reflects a similar fascination. When I was first invited to prepare the conference talks that became the embryonic version of this book, I did a quick spot of unscientific research on the website of my local Christian book shop, which reinforced my suspicions about the scale of the contemporary Christian leadership-fixation. Type "leader" into the search engine of their catalogue and you get no less than 1243 results; that compares with 697 for "teacher," 489 for "pastor," 285 for "missionary," 192 for "disciple," 176 for "minister," 158 for "servant," 51 for "evangelist," 36 for "elder" and 25 for "administrator." It would be foolish to place too much reliance on the findings of my little three-minute research project. And there are some obvious reasons, too,

2. Kellerman, *The End of Leadership*, xiii.

3. Ibid., 156.

4. Ibid., 154.

why the generic, contemporary, secular-sounding word "leadership" might trump the more particular, archaic, religiously-flavored or denomination-ally-specific alternatives in the language that we choose to use for the titles of our books and the wording of our mission statements. But it's striking, nevertheless, that it is *this* generic word that we instinctively reach for; that it is underneath the concepts of "leaders" and "leadership" that we choose to organize our thinking.

And yet, when you go looking in the Bible, you realize pretty quickly that it's a word that can hardly be found there at all. The Bible certainly contains a host of concrete instances of individuals, tasks, offices, and images that you might want to connect in some way with the category of leaders and leadership: mothers, fathers, shepherds, sages, prophets, judges, priests, kings, messiahs, apostles, pastors, elders, overseers . . . the instances are everywhere. But the abstraction, the umbrella term "leadership," hardly rates a mention.

A situation like that, in which there is a key organizing concept that is everywhere in the language of Christians but hardly present in the language of Scripture, suggests an obvious danger. The danger is that we will take the generic concept "leadership," whose meaning we think we already know (because our culture—not just our secular culture but our *Christian* culture—tells us what it means) and impose that concept uncritically onto the various gifts and tasks and offices and images in the Bible with which we connect it. And because the concept is such a ubiquitous one, and one that is so highly prized and celebrated, a distortion here can be particularly seductive and particularly damaging.

More than that. Good leadership, as we shall see, is meant to be a vector, pointing toward something other than itself, and an act of service, promoting interests other than its own. The kind of leadership that is fostered in a leadership-fixated culture will almost inevitably be forgetful of these things, even when it pays lip-service to them. Good leadership is much less interested in itself than it is in the people whom it seeks to lead and the destination toward which it seeks to lead them. There will always be a place for the occasional book or conference or course focusing on leadership itself—on the qualities and techniques of an effective leader. But the more such books and conferences and courses proliferate, the more they need to be matched by a different sort of leadership-discourse: the sort that deliberately places the theme of leadership off-center and out-of-focus, orienting it toward the ends which it ought to serve and locating it within the relationships in which it ought to belong.

That is why I ended up saying yes to the conference invitation and to the idea of writing this book—not so much *despite* the fact that there is such a vast quantity of Christian books and courses and conferences on leadership as (paradoxically) *because* of that fact. When a particular topic has come to dominate the conversation of a culture, disproportionately and distortingly, one possible response is simply to change the conversation— to move away to another corner of the room and start talking loudly and enthusiastically about something else.[5] Sometimes that works. But it still leaves unanswered the question of why the original conversation evolved the way it did, and it does nothing to point the way to how the topic of that original conversation could better be understood. In such circumstances, wisdom requires not only a fresh conversation but also a patient, critical, positive participation in the original one, with the aim of understanding it better and moving it to where it ought to be. That is the purpose that I hope this book will serve.

So my task in this book includes both the job of understanding what it is in us and in our culture that wants to elevate and fetishize this abstraction, "leadership," and the job of reconstructing the concept itself (along with the various gifts and tasks and offices that are connected with it) in the light of the gospel. In other words, the task of this book is both critical and constructive. There is a distorted way of seeing leadership that we need to understand and dismantle, but that's only half the job done; the other half is to put it back together again—to reassemble it in a way that retains all the elements of common sense and common grace but organizes those things around the gospel of the Lord Jesus, and subjects them to the wisdom of his word. In other words, my hope is that this book will help you see both what leadership is *not* (or what it ought not to be) and what it *is* (or what it ought to be) in the light of what God has done for us and said to us in Christ.

Unpacking a metaphor

But first things first. What do we mean by "leadership"? Is it possible to give the term at least a basic definition at the start of our discussion? One of the

---

5. Cf. Bruce Winter's comments on the reasons why he placed a blanket ban on the language of "leadership" at the College in which he served as principal. Winter, "Culture's Challenge," 8.

problems with defining leadership in our contemporary cultural context is the aura that the word has around it, which magnifies its attractiveness and the general perception of its importance, without necessarily doing much to clarify its content. The words "leader" and "leadership" carry with them connotations of giftedness, preeminence, status, and position, all of which can be connected at times with leaders and leadership but none of which is at the heart of what the concept is about. Those phenomena are certainly part of the aura that surrounds the concept, but they are not its essence.[6]

For the purposes of the discussion in this book, I will be assuming a definition of leadership that finds the heart of the concept in the metaphor that the word implies: a leader is someone who does (or is asked to do) the job of going somewhere, and taking others with them. A leader proposes a direction, steers a course, and motivates people to move and keep on moving toward a destination. Leadership, then, is a concept that has to do with *direction* and *motivation*. A leader serves a group that he or she belongs to,[7] by taking an active and deliberate role in framing and articulating the group's purposes and strategies,[8] and helping to motivate its members toward the fulfilment of those purposes and the implementation of those strategies.[9]

---

6. At times, of course, it can be precisely one of these related meanings that a person has in mind when the word "leadership" is used. If I were writing a piece of purely descriptive lexicography—composing the dictionary entry that catalogues the various meanings that "leadership" can have in contemporary usage—I would have no good reason to distinguish as I do here between the "aura" of the concept and its "essence." But if it is *concepts* that we are interested in, rather than merely the words that serve as labels or shorthands for them, then it is worth trying to frame a definition more precise and focused than the broad, blurry range of meanings that can be included within the semantic field of a particular English word.

7. In specifying that a leader serves a group "that he or she belongs to," I am seeking to distinguish between a leader and an external consultant, who may assist in framing the purposes and strategies of a group, but does not travel the journey with them in implementing the strategies and fulfilling the purposes. (An outsider to the group may, likewise, contribute in some way to the group's motivation, but that does not make the person a "leader" of the group.)

8. In placing the emphasis of the definition on how leadership relates to the purpose of a group, I have intentionally restricted the scope of its applicability to groups that have (or ought to have) a common purpose of some sort; cf. the arguments in favor of a focus on "purposive social systems" (including groups as small as dyads and as large as whole organizations) as the domain in which leadership operates, in Hackman, "Leadership," 107.

9. A further distinction that the definition hints at, therefore, is the distinction between a leader and an advisor. An advisor (from within or outside the group) like a

One vivid illustration of the directive dimension of leadership is implied by the expression Paul uses in 1 Cor 12:28, which is translated in the English of the NRSV as "forms of leadership." The Greek word Paul uses here (*kybernēsis*) is a metaphorical term, derived originally from the word for the helmsman of a ship (cf. Acts 27:11, Rev 18:17), and adopted in the political discourse of ancient Greece as a conventional image for the task of steering the affairs of a city or a kingdom.[10] Plato, for example, famously depicted the philosopher-king as the ideal "pilot" (*kybernētēs*) for the ship of state, because he is the one who is best equipped to "give his attention to the time of the year, the seasons, the sky, the winds, the stars, and all that pertains to his art," in order to "be a true ruler of a ship."[11] In the Greek translation of the Old Testament (e.g., LXX Prov 11:14; 24:6) the word was used with a similar metaphorical sense to refer to the "guidance" (*kybernēsis*) provided to a nation or army by a wise counsellor (or rather—with an explicit and emphatic plurality—by "an abundance of counsellors").

But offering wise counsel and direction is only half the job of a leader—at least on the definition of the concept that I will be assuming. A leader contributes not only to the wisdom of the group but also to its courage and fortitude, motivating the group's members to embark on a journey in the direction that wisdom suggests, and to persevere in it. To extend the nautical metaphor a little further, leadership involves both standing at the helm to steer a course and persuading (or commanding, or inspiring) the crew to man the rigging or pull the oars.

While it is important to attempt some sort of definition of what we mean by the concept of leadership, it would be a mistake to draw the

---

leader, plays a part in clarifying purposes and framing strategies, but a leader's role also includes some measure of involvement in the more public role of motivating the group toward the fulfilment of its purposes and the implementation of its strategies.

10. The fact that the word originally referred to the helmsman of a ship does not, in and of itself, prove that it continued to be understood as a nautical metaphor when it was used in leadership contexts in later centuries. In the case of the word *kybernēsis*, however, its use within an extended nautical metaphor in a text as prominent and influential as Plato's *Republic* and the continuing appeals to the metaphor in the Greek political literature of the subsequent centuries combine to suggest that readers and listeners in Paul's time would have still been aware of the nautical background of the term when it was used to refer to leadership roles in non-nautical contexts.

11. Plato, *Republic* 6.488d. Cf. the similar metaphor in Dio Chrysostom, *Discourses* 48.14, and Polybius's description of a legitimate monarchy as one that is voluntarily accepted and "governed" (*kybernōmenēn*) by an appeal to reason rather than to fear or force (*Histories* 6.4.2).

boundary lines too tightly, or to imagine that leaders come in only one shape and size. Because of the wide range of contexts in which leadership is exercised, the differing proportions in which the directive and motivational functions of leadership can be combined, and the varying modes in which those functions can be fulfilled, leadership (even within my own somewhat restrictive definition) can take many different forms. Paul's own passing reference to "varieties of leadership" (*kybernēseis*, in the plural) offers a hint in this direction. But it is still possible, even when ample room has been left open for that variety of forms and contexts, to identify a core concept that can be defined with some clarity.

Some clarifications and distinctions

A few very simple Venn diagrams may clarify how this understanding of leadership relates to several other related concepts.

(i) Leadership and authority

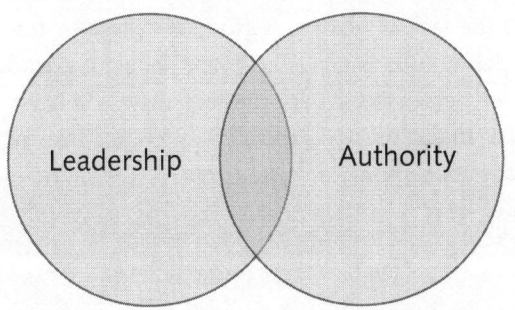

If leadership means giving a group of people direction and motivation in a journey toward a destination, then not all leadership involves an exercise of authority, and not all authority is directed toward the task of leadership. It is possible to take initiative in proposing a course of action and to convince others to follow it, without possessing any particular authority within the group. A leader may win the consent of the group by appealing to some authority external to himself or herself, or may simply fill a vacuum that has been created by the absence of any alternative proposal. Conversely, a person may possess authority without providing (or being expected to provide) leadership. A person's authority may, for example, relate to the allocation of resources or the preservation of tradition or the custodianship of knowledge, rather than to the task of leadership *per se*. The overlap between leadership and authority is certainly substantial, but it is not total.

(ii) Leaders and office-bearers

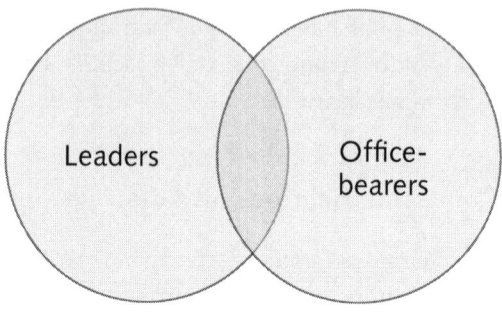

If leadership and authority are overlapping but not identical circles, the same can be said of the categories of leaders and office-bearers. A group may appoint people to all sorts of offices of responsibility, only some of which involve the task of leading a group in a task or toward a destination. A financial auditor is an office-bearer but not a leader; conversely, a charismatic or persuasive group-member may be a leader without ever being appointed to any office. Leadership and office-bearing frequently go together, but the concepts are not identical.

(iii) Leaders and teachers

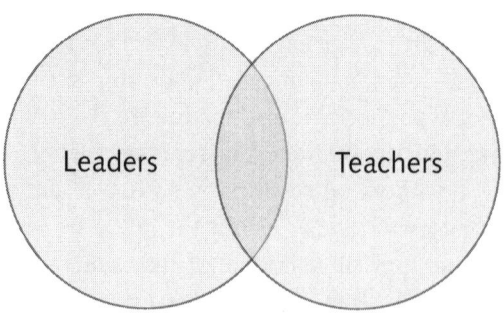

The relationship between leading and teaching is similarly complicated. A person can lead by teaching, passing on to a community of learners the vision, ethos, motivation, skills, and knowledge required for the accomplishment of a mission or the completion of a journey. As we will see in the following chapters, this kind of leading-by-teaching is a crucial aspect of the particular shape that leadership ought to take within the Christian church. But not all leaders are teachers—some (for example) lead simply by naked command, or the threat of force, or personal charisma, or perceived trustworthiness. In a football team, the captain and the coach are both leaders, but it is usually only the coach whose leadership takes the form of teaching. Equally, not all teachers are leaders—some teachers are given the job of developing students in knowledge, skills, or attitudes that bear no obvious or necessary relationship with any mission or journey, except to the extent that the learning is viewed as an end in itself.

(iv) Leadership and servanthood

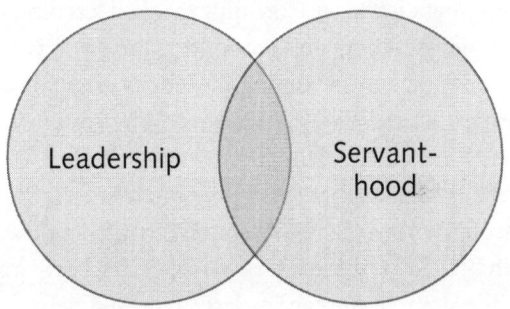

Finally, a word should be said about the overlapping categories of leadership and servanthood. If the defining quality of servants is that they seek not their own advantage but the advantage of others, then it could certainly be argued that genuinely Christian leadership—indeed *all* good leadership—takes the form of "servant-leadership." But that is not because of some quality intrinsic to the definition of leadership. Leadership can be oppressive and exploitative, and servanthood, conversely, can take many forms other than leadership. The overlap between the two circles is of crucial importance to a Christian theology of leadership and ministry, but each of the two concepts needs first to be understood in its own right before the nature of their overlap can be properly grasped.

This, then, is the working definition that I will be assuming for the purposes of this book: *leadership is the act or task of making an intentional contribution toward the direction and motivation of a group in the framing and pursuit of a common purpose.*[12] The concept of leadership, understood according to this definition, is thus closely related to but distinguishable from the concepts of authority, office, teaching, and servanthood.

Why 1 Corinthians?

If that is what I will be taking "leadership" to mean, my aim in this book is (as I said earlier in this chapter) a double one: (i) to understand the distortions in our practice of leadership and our thinking about it that take place when it is isolated and idolized as an end in itself, and (ii) to reorient it toward the ends which it ought to serve, when it is understood in the light of the gospel. As a method for attempting that task, my plan is not to cast my gaze across the whole of the Bible and attempt some kind of giant synthesis. Instead, I will be adopting the less ambitious approach of zeroing in on one New Testament letter—1 Corinthians—and learning from how Paul does the job of understanding and reorienting the notions and practices of leadership that have taken root among the letter's original readers.

This approach needs some justification. Why concentrate on just one book of the Bible, and this book in particular? After all, 1 Corinthians does not really advertise itself as a leadership manual. In fact, the word "leadership" hardly occurs within the whole sixteen chapters of the letter. On one occasion (in the NRSV translation of 1 Cor 3:21) Paul urges the Corinthians not to "boast about human leaders," but even here a quick check of the original language reveals that the phrase "about human leaders" is the NRSV's interpretive expansion of the Greek *en anthrōpois* ("in humans").[13]

---

12. I have omitted from the definition any explicit reference to the role that leaders play in shaping the *ethos* of a group. This is not because I think it is unimportant, but because: (i) in some groups (e.g., a small team of students working together on a short-term group project), the shaping of ethos is incidental rather than essential to the task of leadership; and, more importantly, (ii) in a group like the church, the shaping of ethos is included within the pursuit of the common purpose for which the church exists and implied by the metaphorical destination toward which it is travelling. These issues are explored further in chapter 3, below.

13. Within the context of 1 Cor 3–4, it is clear that the primary form of "boasting in humans" that Paul is seeking to correct is the Corinthians' boasting in leaders and teachers like himself and Apollos, so there is some good contextual justification for the NRSV's way of rendering the immediate force of Paul's words into English.

That instance aside, the one place that the word "leadership" is used in 1 Corinthians is a fleeting reference to "forms of leadership" in 12:28, tucked in between "forms of assistance" and "various kinds of tongues," within a list of gifts with which God has blessed the body of Christ. "Leadership" can scarcely be said to occupy the central place within 1 Corinthians as the organizing concept around which the letter has been written.

Nevertheless, in the course of the letter, Paul finds himself dealing with a whole cluster of issues closely connected with what I have defined as "leadership." At various points, among and in connection with the other themes that the letter addresses, Paul writes to the Corinthians at some length about issues of wisdom, power, honor, status, giftedness, authority, purpose, and example. Even at the points of the letter where these leadership-related themes are not in view, Paul is still exercising a kind of leadership himself, within a letter in which he repeatedly and explicitly calls attention to his own apostleship and teaching ministry as in some sense exemplary and paradigmatic (e.g., 3:21—4:7; 9:1—11:1). And all of this takes place, as a number of commentators have argued, in a context within which Paul's own leadership credentials have been called into question,[14] partly at least because of the distorted, "Corinthianized" understandings of leadership and leadership-related issues, which the Corinthians have absorbed from the mindset of the surrounding culture.

Thus, while 1 Corinthians is not a Pauline leadership manual, it is (one could argue) something even more useful for our current purposes than that. It is an inspired, canonical case study—a worked example of what is involved in the complicated task of disentangling the various components of leadership from the cultural matrix in which they have come to be understood, in order to reorient them toward their proper end. Given the aims of this book, 1 Corinthians is an ideal part of the canon to focus on.

The Corinthianization of Leadership

To speak of the "Corinthianized" understandings of leadership that Paul is addressing within his letter, or of the "Corinthianization" of Christian leadership, as I have in the heading of this section, is to make use of words that are ugly in more ways than one. Within the ancient world, "Corinthianization" was not a concept with polite connotations. In the classical period, going back at least as far as Aristophanes, the verb *korinthiazesthai* meant "to

14. See especially Fee, *First Corinthians*, 4–15.

fornicate," a colloquialism that traded on the reputation of Greek Corinth for sexual promiscuity, and the connotations of the word would not have lost their currency in Paul's day.[15] The sense in which I am using the word here, in speaking of the "Corinthianization" of Christian leadership, is not the same as that, but it is a metaphorical extension of it; perhaps the closest equivalent from our own era would be the way in which the Red Hot Chilli Peppers sang about the "Californication" of imagination and desire inflicted on the world by the dream-factories of Hollywood. The "Corinthianization" of leadership is the uncritical absorption and imitation of the mindset and power-structures of the surrounding culture—particularly the kind of mindset and power-structures that were prominent and influential in first-century Roman Corinth. It is, I think, what Paul is referring to in his warning in 2 Corinthians against being "unequally yoked with unbelievers" (2 Cor 6:14) and in the graphic sexual and cultic metaphors with which he illustrates the concept within the immediately following verses and later in the letter (2 Cor 6:14—7:1; 11:1–4).[16]

Within the Corinthian church, this uncritical absorption of cultural values alien to the gospel took a distressingly blatant and shocking form. Within his letters to them, Paul expresses his bewilderment at the extent to which they have come to exhibit what he would expect of "people of the flesh," rather than "spiritual people" (1 Cor 3:1). And the ethos of Roman Corinth (even when due allowance is made for the somewhat jaundiced perspective of outside observers) was a particularly crass version of what Paul describes as "the mind of the flesh" and "the wisdom of the world." The Athenian writer Alciphron, for example, has no time for Corinth, expressing his distaste at "the sordidness of the rich there and the misery of the poor," and Dio Chrysostom (from Prusa in Bithynia) paints a picture of a flashy, shallow, carnivalesque Corinthian public square: "That was the time, too, when one could hear crowds of wretched sophists around Poseidon's temple shouting and reviling one another, and their disciples, as they were called, fighting with one another, many writers reading aloud their stupid

---

15. Aristophanes, *Fragments* 354; Plato used the expression *korinthia korē* (Corinthian girl) to mean "prostitute" (*Republic*, 404d) and Philetaerus and Poliochus both wrote plays called *Korinthiastēs*, "The Whore-Monger" (Athenaeus, *The Learned Banqueters* 313c, 559a). According to Strabo, who was writing in the first century AD, the memory of Greek Corinth was still alive in his own time, and the saying "Not for every man is the voyage to Corinth" continued to be used of Roman Corinth in his own day: Strabo, *Geography* 8.6.20. Cf. Murphy-O'Connor, *St Paul's Corinth*, 56–57.

16. I have argued for this view in Starling, "The Apistoi of 2 Cor. 6:14," 1–17.

works, many poets reciting their poems while others applauded them, many jugglers showing their tricks, many fortune tellers interpreting fortunes, lawyers innumerable perverting judgement, and peddlers not a few peddling whatever they happened to have."[17]

But the mindset and mores that influenced the Corinthian church, while not identical to those of the modern West, bear some striking resemblances to the culture of our time. Anthony Thiselton, for example, highlights a string of phenomena in the culture of first-century Corinth that constitute striking points of contact between the Corinthian Christians' circumstances and our own.[18] Nor should we be naïve about the extent to which we ourselves, as Christians, are liable to uncritically absorbing them in the way we think and act in all matters, including the matter of how we understand and practice leadership. The Corinthians are—in some powerfully illuminating ways—our contemporaries, and we would do well to pay close attention to how Paul responds to the ways in which they have "Corinthianized" the practices of Christian leadership, so that we can be alert to the parallel tendencies in our own situation.

This book

My plan in this book, therefore, is to direct our attention to the ways in which Paul exposes the leadership and leadership-related concepts that the Corinthian church had imported from their culture, critiques them in the light of the message of the cross and resurrection, and teaches and demonstrates what leadership ought to look like for those who believe the gospel. Exploring one dimension at a time, my intention is to work through various aspects of the meaning of leadership and the tasks and resources that it involves, looking first at the Corinthian version of those aspects of leadership, then at the very unCorinthian corrective that Paul brings to bear in his teaching and his example, and then applying that corrective and that positive vision for leadership to our own context today.

17. Alciphron, *Letters* 3.24; Dio Chrysostom *Discourses* 8.9. (While the description in the latter is set in the context of a narration of the life of Diogenes, it is generally agreed that it is heavily colored by the impressions that Dio had formed of Corinth in his own day. Cf. Jones, *The Roman World of Dio Chrysostom*, 47–49.)

18. Thiselton, *First Corinthians*, 16–17. Thiselton's list includes such phenomena as "status inconsistency," "religious pluralism," "cosmopolitan immigration and trade," and "priority of market forces not only in business but also in rhetoric."

Readers who are familiar with the (massive) body of contemporary literature on Christian leadership will notice its almost complete absence from the text and footnotes of this book. This is not because I regard it as without value, but because I am not sufficiently familiar with it to interact intelligently with its strengths and weaknesses—I will leave it to others to do that job better than I can. Nor have I filled the book with real-life examples of "Corinthian" behavior by contemporary churches and Christian leaders, or piles of studies and statistics to prove how prevalent such practices are. I am confident that readers can quite readily call to mind examples from their own experience and observation; if that is not the case for some readers, then I am delighted to hear it! Equally, while the book contains the occasional more encouraging example of "unCorinthian" practices past and present, these are comparatively few in number; most of the time I have left it to the reader to do the sort of work that Paul commends in Philippians 3—to find examples of people in his or her own context who "live according to the example you have in us," and use them not as distant heroes to admire but as close-up examples to emulate.

The book as a whole will not add up to a mini-commentary on 1 Corinthians, though I hope that readers will learn something along the way about the letter and its original context. Nor will it amount to a systematic how-to manual on the art of leadership, though my desire is that readers' understanding of leadership will be deepened and enriched by it. Instead, it will take the form of a series of reflections, starting in each case with a portion of Paul's letter to the Corinthians, and pondering its implications for a particular aspect of how we ought to understand and practice Christian leadership in our contemporary context. For readers who are studying 1 Corinthians, my intention is that the book will stimulate thought on the implications of the letter for the practice of Christian leadership; for readers who are studying Christian leadership or serving as leaders within the church, my intention is that the book will provoke inquiry into the biblical and theological roots of a distinctively Christian understanding of the task. Either way, the book is intended as a kind of bridge between the text of 1 Corinthians and the task of Christian leadership. My prayer is that it will contribute to the work of raising up and sustaining a generation of humble, wise, bold, faithful, unCorinthian leaders for the churches of today and tomorrow.

two

THE KINGDOM,
THE POWER AND THE GLORY

1 CORINTHIANS 3:18 — 4:21

The essential unity of the First Epistle to the Corinthians is a quite specific criticism which Paul applies to the Christian Church. He reproaches it with the fact that the human, the vital, the heroic or even colossal, the individual arbitrary elements which are mixed up in Christianity, as in every other human phenomenon, are in the process of growing with rank luxuriance, and becoming an end in themselves . . . And in this he now perceives not only a danger but *the* danger. For what is at stake in Christianity is the rule of God and nothing else.[1]

The Glory

The culture of first-century Corinth was, like our own, a leadership-fixated culture. More precisely, it was a culture fixated on the aura of eminence and glory and status that surrounds the concept of leadership and the person of a leader. In first-century Corinth, at every level of society, the practice of leadership was inextricably connected with status, honor, and glory. The pattern was set right at the top of the tree, in Rome, and it was reduplicated

---

1. Barth, *The Resurrection of the Dead*, 103–4.

locally among the elite of the city. For them, the official civic leadership roles were not so much about functions and job descriptions as they were about hierarchies of prestige and standing. If you held an office of leadership there were usually some responsibilities and duties involved, but as much as that—or more so in the case of some roles—a leadership position functioned and was understood as a badge of honor. Thus, the civic positions to which you could be appointed to were arranged in an elaborate *cursus honorum*—a ladder of status levels. They went with special dress codes and special seats on public occasions, and they carried the expectation that you would contribute some of your wealth toward public buildings and games and festivals, and have it recorded that you had done so in the form of public inscriptions and statues.[2]

Writing late in the first century or early in the second, the philosopher and orator Dio Chrysostom speaks about the many people in cities like Corinth who sought high office "not for the sake of what is truly best in the interest of their country itself, but for the sake of reputation and honors and the possession of greater power than their neighbors, in the pursuit of crowns and precedence and purple robes, fixing their gaze upon these things and staking all upon their attainment."[3] "All men," he says in another one of his orations, "set great store by the outward tokens of high achievement ["the pillar, the inscription, and being set up in bronze"] and not one man in a thousand is willing to agree that what he regards as a noble deed shall have been done for himself alone and that no other man shall have knowledge of it."[4]

That was the pattern at the top of the tree. And the same pattern continued all the way down the ladder to the trade guilds and the burial societies and the household *collegia*. At every level there were the same carefully defined and articulated hierarchies of honor and status, often with exactly the same titles that were used for the elites of the city: *magister, curator, decurion, quaestor, archiereus,* and so on.[5] The language and structures of leadership in Jewish circles were notably similar to those that could be found among the pagans. The records left behind by the synagogues of the Greek and Roman cities testify to a whole array of leadership positions (*archōn, archisynagōgos, gerousiarch, prostatis, patēr synagōgēs,*

2. Cf. Lendon, *Empire of Honour*, 1–29; MacMullen, *Roman Social Relations*, 105–8.

3. Dio Chrysostom, *Discourses* 34.29.

4. Dio Chrysostom, *Discourses* 31.20, 22.

5. See especially Clarke, *Serve the Community of the Church*, 35–77.

matēr synagōgēs) bestowed as honors on the wealthy and well-born and prestigious.[6] The overall picture conveyed by the evidence that survives from the period suggests that the exercise of leadership (and the aspiration to its exercise) in a city like Roman Corinth involved a constant, pervasive, deliberate competition for honors that were purchased and fought over and publicly displayed.

Boasting

That is the context in which the "boasting" that Paul talks about in the opening chapters of 1 Corinthians was taking place. In a society that was elaborately organized into gradations of glory, you boasted in order to gain honor and you boasted in turn about the honor you had gained.

It's not that different in our own modern, Western context, of course. The anthropologists speak about "honor-shame" cultures as if ours were not one, but the quest for honor and the concealment of shame are not motivations that are entirely alien to us, even if our own hierarchies of status and reputation and honor are configured a little differently and calibrated on another scale. The individualism of modern Western cultures, for example, diminishes the extent to which the honoring and shaming of the group is shared among its members, the pyramid of wealth and status is significantly less steep in most modern cultures than it was in the world of the first century,[7] and the reverence for age and tradition that stands behind the values of most honor-shame cultures has been greatly eroded in our own. But anxieties about social status and a concern for image and reputation are no less present in us than in our ancestors. David DeSilva, describing his own North American context, observes: "Typically we do not talk about honor and shame much . . . but we do wrestle with 'worth,' with 'self-esteem,' with the push and pull of 'what other people will think.' The vocabulary has greatly receded, but the dynamics are still very much present. We want to know that we are valuable, worthwhile people, and we want to give the impression of being such."[8]

In my own Australian culture, similar observations could be made. We pride ourselves on how much less overt our boasting is than the boasting that is permitted and encouraged in some other cultures, but we're

---

6. Cf. ibid., 103–41.

7. Cf. MacMullen, *Roman Social Relations*, 88–97.

8. DeSilva, *Honor, Patronage, Kinship & Purity*, 26.

hardly unique in that respect—Plutarch back in the first century wrote a whole manual on "How one can praise oneself without arousing envy"—and we still find a way to let the news of our achievements leak out so we can get the glory for them.

And for the Corinthians—as is the case with us—the boasting that people did was not just about their own accomplishments and abilities but also about the people with whom they were associated. There was a kind of reflected glory, a status by association, that came with being connected to the right person, part of the right crowd, accepted in the right group. So Paul says in 1 Cor 1:11–12, "it has been reported to me by Chloe's people that there are quarrels among you, my brothers and sisters. What I mean is that each of you says, 'I belong to Paul,' or 'I belong to Apollos,' or 'I belong to Cephas,' or 'I belong to Christ.'" He describes it in 3:21 as "boasting about human leaders," and in 4:6 as being "puffed up in favor of one against another." Like the "disciples" of the sophists that Dio Chrysostom depicts as "shouting and reviling one another" in front of Poseidon's temple, the Corinthians were questing after glory for themselves by championing the excellencies of the teachers to whom they had (wisely, discerningly, meritoriously) attached themselves.[9]

In our own time the scope for this sort of boasting—both in our own accomplishments and in the accomplishments of others—has been magnified a thousand-fold through the mirror-lenses of the internet. Self-promotion and celebrity-adulation are nothing new, but the internet has given us a whole new screen onto which we can project our faces and a whole new capacity to broadcast our praises and plaudits to the world (or, at least, to that portion of the world that pays attention to our posts and pictures and status updates).[10] We are no strangers to the boasting game.

The end of boasting

The opening chapters of 1 Corinthians launch a devastating assault against the culture of boasting that had taken root within the church in Corinth. Paul's concern within these chapters is not only with the divisions the boasting contest engendered, but also with the arrogance and folly they

---

9. See especially Winter, *After Paul Left Corinth*, 31–43; and Pickett, *The Cross in Corinth*, 39–58.

10. Cf. Carpenter, "Narcissism on Facebook," 482–86; Twenge and Campbell, *The Narcissism Epidemic*, 107–22.

expressed. And as this first section of the letter draws toward its climax, in 1 Cor 3:18—4:7, Paul offers the Corinthians a string of reasons why there ought to be no room for that sort of competitive boasting among the people of God.

(I) BOASTING AND WISDOM (3:18–21)

The first reason Paul offers has to do with the foolishness that boasting of this sort exhibits: "Do not deceive yourselves. If you think that you are wise in this age, you should become fools so that you may become wise. For the wisdom of this world is foolishness with God. For it is written, 'He catches the wise in their craftiness,' and again, 'The Lord knows the thoughts of the wise, that they are futile.' So let no one boast about human leaders" (3:18–21).

The mindset that boasts in precedence and honor, jockeys for position, and ranks people in order of their status—that whole mindset, Paul says, is part of the wisdom of an age that is passing away, and it is foolishness with God. In the message of the cross, God has made known a different wisdom; God has made himself known as the one who exalts the humble, delights in the servant, brings down the proud, chooses the things that are not, and reduces to nothing the things that are.

The implications for us are obvious and far-reaching: when we boast in the great speakers and the gifted leaders and the beautiful and the intelligent, when we jostle to be among them or to be close to them—and when we trade on such motivations in the way we market and promote our ministries—we exhibit exactly the kind of "wisdom" that God's whole plan of salvation is calculated to destroy. Oratory, leadership, beauty and intelligence (as Paul goes on to imply in 4:7) are all good gifts from God, to be delighted in and enjoyed with thanksgiving to him. That is wisdom. But *boasting* in such things (whether our own or those of others) and ranking people in status hierarchies according to their possession of them is not wisdom but foolishness in the sight of God. It is a foolishness that sets itself up against God; a foolishness that God, in turn, has solemnly promised to destroy.

(II) BOASTING AND BELONGING (3:21–23)

One dimension of the foolishness exhibited in such boasting (as Paul goes on to argue in verses 21–23), is the way in which it misunderstands what *belonging* means within God's people and within God's world: "So let no one boast about human leaders," Paul writes. "For all things are yours, whether Paul or Apollos or Cephas or the world or life or death or the present or the future—all belong to you, and you belong to Christ, and Christ belongs to God."

To treat leaders like celebrities, arguing over which is the greatest and dividing into factions according to our various allegiances to the one or the other, is to act as if we had to pick just one of them to own or to belong to. In reality, however, Paul reminds us that they already belong to us, as our servants—all of them, to all of us; and we belong to Christ, and Christ belongs to God. The world as Paul depicts it in these verses is not a big pile of status tokens for us to anxiously compete over; it all belongs to God, and he graciously shares it with whomever he chooses. And all the glory is his—"you belong to Christ, and Christ belongs to God"—so you and I are set free from the wearisome contests that beset the lives of those who are dedicated to amassing glory for themselves. We can take a deep breath, relax and remember that all things are from God and for him, and there are no bragging rights that we need (or are entitled) to fight over.

(III) BOASTING AND JUDGMENT (4:1–5)

If "you belong to Christ, and Christ belongs to God," then, thirdly (as Paul goes on to assert in 4:1–5), boasting in human leaders shows that we haven't understood whose servants they are, ultimately, and whose judgment about them really matters. Paul writes:

> Think of us in this way, as servants of Christ and stewards of God's mysteries. Moreover, it is required of stewards that they be found trustworthy. But with me it is a very small thing that I should be judged by you or by any human court. I do not even judge myself. I am not aware of anything against myself, but I am not thereby acquitted. It is the Lord who judges me. Therefore do not pronounce judgment before the time, before the Lord comes, who will bring to light the things now hidden in darkness and will disclose the purposes of the heart. Then each one will receive commendation from God.

Human leaders, Paul insists, are servants, "slaves" even.[11] And while they serve the church, they are principally and ultimately slaves of Christ, accountable to him. When we measure and compare leaders and speakers as if they were the performers and we were the fans or the judges in the talent show, we misconceive entirely what the true judgment is—the only one that is of eternal consequence. And those of us who are leaders and teachers ourselves need to remember that the one whose evaluation and opinion ultimately count for something is the one who sees the hidden things and the purposes of the heart.

(IV) BOASTING AND SCRIPTURE (4:6)

These perspectives are not plucked by Paul out of the air, or borrowed from the pagan philosophers; nor are they brand-new, first-century Christian inventions. They go back deep into the wisdom of the Old Testament Scriptures, as Paul has already demonstrated in the way that he has laced the preceding chapters with scriptural quotations and allusions. If that is the case, then (according to the conclusion Paul draws in 4:6) boasting in human cleverness and greatness and wisdom shows an arrogant failure on our part to submit our hearts to the word of God in Scripture, to humble ourselves and sit under what God says.[12] Paul writes: "I have applied all this to Apollos and myself for your benefit, brothers and sisters, so that you may learn through us the meaning of the saying, 'Nothing beyond what is written,' so that none of you will be puffed up in favor of one against another." If the path to knowing God were via human cleverness and charisma, then the clever ones and the charismatic ones would be the ones to lift up and glorify. But if leaders and teachers are just "stewards of God's mysteries," then there's no such thing as a "great Bible teacher" or a "great Christian speaker," however much we may want to imply the contrary in the blurbs for our books and the posters for our conferences. The place of the teacher is not the place of greatness—dispensing their deep wisdom and exhibiting their impressive personality. The place of the teacher is the low, humble place of the one who has nothing beyond what it is written, who is simply a servant of the Word.

11. See especially the discussion in Harris, *Slave of Christ*, 127–56.
12. Cf. Hays, *First Corinthians,* 68–69.

(v) Boasting and Grace (4:7)

This does not mean that the gifts of speakers and teachers and leaders are to be despised or devalued as worthless—after all, Paul himself commences the letter in 1:5–7 with an expression of enthusiastic thankfulness to God for the way in which the Corinthian church has been "enriched in [Christ Jesus] in speech and knowledge of every kind . . . so that you are not lacking in any spiritual gift." The point is that gifts (whether gifts of speech or teaching or leadership, or any other gift) are to be received as *gifts*. Boasting in "leadership"—or any other kind of boasting that's not at its root an expression of delight in God and gratitude to him—forgets God's grace: "What do you have that you did not receive? And if you received it, why do you boast as if it were not a gift?"

Paul's rebuke has implications both for the private boasting that we engage in as individuals and for the larger economy and culture of our churches.[13] The marketing-driven ethos of the modern Western consumerist church, with its competitive self-promotion and its commodification of the gifts of God, amounts—to the extent that we buy into it—to a denial of grace every bit as serious as the indulgence-trafficking of the medieval church. In the short term, if people are buying our products, attending our conventions, and liking our status updates, it may feel good. But in the long term, even when it is succeeding, it still fails, because it leaches out the sweetness from the product that it sells. It turns preaching from an announcement that points away from itself toward the grace of God into a performance that asks to be admired and a product that asks to be purchased. And it turns the church from a community that delights together in God's goodness into a business that sells its products in the marketplace. Paul's assault on Christian boasting is strong medicine, but it is medicine nonetheless, and medicine that we need to take in large doses.

Image

Hand in hand with the Corinthians' boasting in leaders and leadership went their obsession with image, and with their place and reputation in society. Greco-Roman culture was a pervasively visual culture, in which

---

13. Cf. the critiques in Wells, *The Courage to be Protestant*, 23–58; Milbank, "Stale Expressions," 264—78; and Stevenson, *Brand Jesus*, 142–59.

status was visibly evident and visually evaluated.[14] "Most men," observes the Greek historian Plutarch, "think themselves robbed of their wealth if they are prevented from displaying it."[15] And the Corinthian Christians— or at least, the elite within the church that Paul is principally addressing in this letter—were deeply conscious of how they appeared and how they were seen by their neighbors.

The exhibited apostles (4:8–17)

Paul responds to this Corinthian obsession with image and appearance with a sharp, rhetorical, fiercely sarcastic reminder of the contrasting exhibition that God had put on display in the apostles. If the Corinthians thought that there was a way of following Jesus and cultivating an impressive image, then they clearly hadn't looked properly at the apostles who had first introduced them to Jesus:

> Already you have all you want! Already you have become rich! Quite apart from us you have become kings! Indeed, I wish that you had become kings, so that we might be kings with you! For I think that God has exhibited us apostles as last of all, as though sentenced to death, because we have become a spectacle to the world, to angels and to mortals. We are fools for the sake of Christ, but you are wise in Christ. We are weak, but you are strong. You are held in honor, but we in disrepute. To the present hour we are hungry and thirsty, we are poorly clothed and beaten and homeless, and we grow weary from the work of our own hands. When reviled, we bless; when persecuted, we endure; when slandered, we speak kindly. We have become like the rubbish of the world, the dregs of all things, to this very day. I am not writing this to make you ashamed, but to admonish you as my beloved children. For though you might have ten thousand guardians in Christ, you do not have many fathers. Indeed, in Christ Jesus I became your father through the gospel. I appeal to you, then, be imitators of me. For this reason I sent you Timothy, who is my beloved and faithful child in the Lord, to remind you of my ways in Christ Jesus, as I teach them everywhere in every church. (4:8–17)

14. Cf. Savage, *Power through Weakness*, 22–23; MacMullen, *Roman Social Relations*, 62, 109.

15. *Marcus Cato* 18.3.

Paul's description of the apostles as "exhibited . . . last of all, as though sentenced to death . . . a spectacle" evokes images of the gladiatorial shows of the Roman theater, and of the triumphal processions that the Romans enacted to honor their returning legions.[16] At the end of the show, at the back of the procession, were the captive slaves and condemned criminals. Their place in the spectacle was to fight and die in the arena, before the eyes of all. The point for the Corinthians is stark and shocking: the place in which God had put their leaders on display before the eyes of the world was not among the glittering company at the front of the procession, or in the best seats of the audience, but at the back of the procession, among those whose lot was to suffer and die. And the Corinthians were called not merely to absorb the shame of being associated them, or to admire their heroism from a distance, but to be "imitators" of them (verse 16). The "spectacle" of apostolic suffering to which Paul refers in verse 9 may be intended by the synagogue rulers and Roman magistrates as nothing more than a ritual of shame and humiliation, but Paul insists that it is not they who are ultimately responsible for staging the show. It is actually *God* who has put the apostles on display, and he has done so (in part, at least) in order that they might serve as an example to be imitated by others, including the Corinthians.

Frequently, of course, the kind of display that is exhibited by Christian leaders looks like something very different from what Paul describes in these verses. I still remember one lunch time, back in my fourth year at University, stepping out of the little crowd at the end of public meeting of the Evangelical Union to go to a lecture, looking back for a moment over my shoulder at the in-group of the EU—the president, the vice-presidents, and their various girlfriends and boyfriends—and being suddenly struck by how *beautiful* they all were. There they were: a little cluster of expensively-educated, fashionably-dressed, good-looking people—a kind of undergraduate Christian Camelot.

There were reasons, of course, for why they looked that way. To start with, there is the fact that this was a university group in a wealthy Western country, so this was hardly a random sample of the global church. Then, in addition, there was the added bias that comes with the eyes of the beholder: they were my friends and I liked them, and they may not have looked so attractive to another observer. But even when all the appropriate allowances have been made, there is still something strange and anomalous about the

16. Cf. Carson, *The Cross and Christian Ministry*, 105; Thiselton, *First Corinthians*, 359–60; Garland, *1 Corinthians*, 140.

picture of that little cluster of the beautiful people, gathered together as the leaders of a group that serves the crucified Jesus.

God is perfectly free to use the wise, the powerful, the nobly-born as leaders among his people, if he so chooses. But the example of the apostles (and the earlier argument in 1 Cor 1:18–31) suggests that if God does choose to do that at times, it is the exception and not the rule. If our thinking is to be shaped by the message of the cross and the example of the apostles, we will need to guard ourselves assiduously against the instinctive human prejudice in favor of the beautiful and the popular, and the instinctive human desire to be counted among them ourselves. That is not the place where real, eternal glory—the glory that matters for the people of Christ—is to be found. God has caused his glory to shine most brightly of all in the face of the crucified Christ; and he loves to show the reflection of that glory in the weak and the despised and the poor and the humble.

That means the kind of leadership that magnifies God's glory is a humble leadership; it's a leadership that does not seek to impress and to be admired; that does not set out to dazzle people with its own wisdom or to gain advantage and position, but devotes itself to the good of others and is willing to be looked down on and criticised and despised. Leadership that is faithful to the word of the cross is not about the pursuit and accumulation of glory.

The Power

And yet, as Paul reminds us in the final verses of the chapter, it is not without power. Sometimes the word "power" can be treated by Christians in our day as if it were a dirty word. We are children of our times, taught by the culture of postmodernity to be deeply suspicious of power and its uses. We tell each other: "leadership is not about power; it's about servanthood."

There is a half-truth buried within our pious denigration of power. The servant of Christ is not a person who pursues power as an end in itself, or manipulates people for his or her own advantage. The message of the cross reminds us that God loves to choose the weak things of this world, and that his power is made perfect in our weakness. And yet it is still his *power* that we are talking about. Any doubts we might have had on that score are removed in the final verses of the chapter: "But some of you, thinking that I am not coming to you, have become arrogant. But I will come to you soon, if the Lord wills, and I will find out not the talk of these arrogant people but their power. For the kingdom of God depends not on talk but on power. What would you prefer? Am I to come to you with a stick, or with love in a spirit of gentleness?" (4:18–21)

Puffed-up Corinthians

The Corinthians, full of their own importance and bloated with the "wisdom" of their superficial cleverness, are described by Paul repeatedly in this letter as "arrogant"—literally "puffed up." They have talk—lots of talk, big words, fancy ideas, grand boasts about spirituality and knowledge and wisdom—but in the end it's just empty talk, hot air.

The Power of Paul's coming (4:18–21)

In contrast (verses 18–21), Paul reminds them of the power of Christ, in which he plans to come to them. He reminds them that where the Kingdom of God is at work—where the rule of God is breaking into this age in the word of the gospel and the work of the Spirit—it creates something more than just talk; more than just hot air. The "whip" he is talking about in verse 21 is a metaphorical whip, of course. But it's a reminder that he is prepared to back up the strong words of his letters with the actions of showing up and confronting the Corinthians face to face. And the reference to Timothy in verse 17 is a reminder that his words about Jesus are backed up by the pattern of a lifestyle that has been shaped by believing what he speaks about.

Evangelicals (myself included) love to talk about words and the Word. We delight in pointing out the way that God can use the words we speak and write, as vehicles of the gospel word, to bring about his purposes in the world. And we rightly do that. But we can forget a little too easily that not all words are powerful. When words are many; when they are bandied around, parroted without conviction, trotted out as empty formulas; when they are nothing more than an entertainment or a display of cleverness; when words are severed from actions—from the work of the Holy Spirit and the fulness of conviction—then they are at risk of remaining nothing more than empty talk. And Paul reminds the Corinthians that empty talk of that kind is not what the Kingdom of God consists in.

The Kingdom

What does leadership look like when it is shaped by and participates in the inbreaking of the Kingdom of God? Three things stand out in this passage as attributes of Kingdom-of-God-shaped leadership.

Not this age but the next

First, according to what Paul says in 3:18–20 and 4:8, Kingdom-of-God-shaped leadership gives its allegiance not to this age but to the next. It acts in this age; it has its feet planted on the ground. But it is directed not by this age's wisdom, and it has no expectation of approval or prestige or fashion-ability in the eyes of this age: "If you think that you are wise in this age, you should become fools so that you may become wise. For the wisdom of this world is foolishness with God" (3:18–19).

Not talk but power

Secondly, as Paul reminds the Corinthians in 4:18–21, Kingdom-of-God-shaped leadership serves the cause of Christ with something more than just talk: "For the kingdom of God depends not on talk but on power" (4:20). There may be a lot of words involved—Bible studies and training seminars and conversations and sermons and books and blog posts, and so on—but they are words that are connected with conviction and with action and with a pattern of life that backs them up.

Not earthly status but divine commendation

Thirdly, as Paul emphasizes in 4:1–5, Kingdom-of-God-shaped leadership seeks not earthly status but divine commendation. It remembers that Jesus is the coming judge, that the status hierarchies of this world will one day be overturned, when "the Lord comes, who will bring to light the things now hidden in darkness and will disclose the purposes of the heart" (4:5). And so it acts boldly and humbly and unassumingly, for the sake of the commendation of God.

All this is particularly problematic for those of us who have been nurtured as leaders within the context of an upper-middle-class Christian youth movement, made up for the most part of articulate, educated, wealthy, young adults who are at a stage of life in which they are surrounded by books and words and ideas. Not all of the readers of this book will come from circumstances like that, but because of the inequalities of wealth, education and access to literature, many will. To learn and to practice leadership in *that* context, in a way that demonstrates that the Kingdom of God consists not just in talk but in the power of God, in full conviction and in courageous action and in transformed lives; to serve within a group where so many are the beautiful and the privileged and the intelligent, and yet to lead in a way that is still not captive to opinion and popularity—that is no easy thing. But if that lesson can be learnt and lived even in a context of that sort—in the Christian colleges and Inter-Varsity Fellowships and suburban young-adult groups of the modern West—then that distinctive aspect of the light of gospel culture will shine out with a sharp, bright contrast. Whatever the context, and whatever the challenges, our prayer must be that God would bless his church with the kind of leaders and servants through whom it may be both declared and demonstrated that the kingdom, the power, and the glory are his, now and forever.

three

DIRECTION

1 CORINTHIANS 9:19 — 11:1

Nothing can wholly satisfy the life of Christ within his followers except the adoption of Christ's purpose toward the world he came to redeem. Fame, pleasure and riches are but husks and ashes in contrast with the boundless and abiding joy of working with God for the fulfillment of his eternal plans.[1]

If, indeed, the goal of Christianity is the imitation of Christ according to the measure of his incarnation . . . they who are entrusted with the guidance of many others are obliged to animate those still weaker than themselves, by their assistance, to the imitation of Christ.[2]

From correction to construction

The task of this book (as I laid it out in the opening chapter) is a double one—both corrective and constructive. The previous chapter was mainly corrective: if the Corinthians' thinking about leadership was focused principally on the aura surrounding the concept—the badges of honor and the pursuit of glory—the gospel reminds us that Kingdom-of-God-shaped

1. J. Campbell White, quoted in Piper, *Desiring God*, 222.
2. Basil, *The Long Rules*, Q43, in *Ascetical Works*, 319.

leadership is not about that. It seeks a glory that is God's, not our own; it travels in the way of sacrifice and service and humility; it does not parade its own wisdom but remembers not to go beyond what is written; it thinks about positions and abilities and leaders as gifts from God, and therefore as nothing to be boasted in; and it has a power that is not the power of bullying or coercion, but the power of God that matches words with conviction and action and example. This chapter—by way of contrast—is focused more on the constructive side of the task. If leadership that understands the gospel is *not* about the pursuit of glory and status and position—if it is not simply a badge of honor to wear—then what *is* it?

Going somewhere

According to the definition sketched out in the introductory chapter, leadership involves giving *direction* and *motivation*—going somewhere, and taking others with you. Leadership implies movement; it's not a static concept but a dynamic one.

Leadership versus Custodianship

In that respect, leadership is different from what you might call custodianship. A custodian stands guard over what is, protecting something precious, keeping it there in its place, warding off any threats. A leader heads off in a direction, and brings other people along for the journey. You can't play "follow the leader" if nobody's moving.

A claim of this sort is, of course, simply a statement about concepts and metaphors. In reality, most roles in the church and the world that we call "leadership" roles involve elements of both leadership and custodianship (and other responsibilities as well). If you're going to take some people from Egypt to the Promised Land, you don't just need a map and a gift for persuasion; you'll also need to need to devote a fair bit of energy to warding off hunger and thirst and mutiny and idolatry and Amorites and Moabites and Amalekites. Nevertheless—whatever other responsibilities that may co-exist with it—there is still built into the concept of "leadership" the idea that there is a cause, a direction, a mission, or a journey to be accomplished. There is no point having leaders if you're not intending to go somewhere.

Gospel mobility

How does that idea translate across to the church, as the principal community in which Christian leadership is exercised? Is "leadership" in that sense the right concept to reach for? Is the church a mobile community, one that is meant to be going somewhere? If we get our bearings from the gospel, then there are at least two crucial senses in which the answer to that question is "yes."

Mission

In the first place, the gospel gives the Christian and the church a momentum toward mission. The gospel message declares that Jesus Christ is Lord of all, that salvation is only in him, for all people, to the ends of the earth; that all authority in heaven and on earth belongs to him, and all people everywhere are summoned to repent and trust him and worship him and delight in him. The unavoidable implication is that the gospel says to the church, and to the individual disciple: "Go." "Go and make disciples of all the nations." The gospel speaks to the church that has become comfortable in itself, within its own cozy ecclesiastical circle, and sends it out into the world, to declare and demonstrate the saving Lordship of Jesus in every corner of the earth.

Pilgrimage

But this momentum into the world in mission is not the only kind of mobility that the gospel imparts to the church. At the same time, equally, the gospel speaks about a coming Kingdom, and constitutes the church as a pilgrim people, as a people on the road toward a destination they haven't arrived at yet, as a people whose home is in another place. The gospel speaks to the church that has gotten comfortable in the world, at home in this present age, and it sets the church on pilgrimage. The picture that best illustrates this second sense of the church's gospel mobility is the picture of Christian in the Pilgrim's Progress, falling asleep in the bower on the slopes of the hill Difficulty, and of the man who comes up behind him and wakes him up and sets him on his way again. As it happens, in Bunyan's version, the man who wakes him speaks with the voice of proverbial wisdom: "Go to the ant, thou sluggard; consider her ways, and be wise." But Bunyan could just as easily have given the part to Evangelist, and taken his lines from Isa 52:1 or Eph 5:14.[3]

The church that is called for by the gospel is a mobile community; it is a community on mission *into* the world, and a community on a pilgrimage *through* the world, toward the life of the coming Kingdom of God.

Corinthian mobility

There is of course another sort of mobility that Christians in our culture are very familiar with—one to which the Corinthians too had a commitment—and that is the upward social mobility of economic and professional and educational advancement. This is the kind of mobility that views the world not as a desert to journey through or a missionfield to reach and bless, but as a ladder to climb. A university, for example, has exactly that meaning for many modern, middle-class Westerners (Christians included). You do your final examinations at the end of high school and you submit your applications, and you wait anxiously for the response that will tell you how many steps up the ladder you can put your foot next. You turn up at university and do your degree (the very word has an etymology that implies a step on a ladder!) and the whole experience functions as a means toward the job and the promotions and the salary and the car and the house and the suburb and the school fees for your children. And on and on the upward path advances, spiraling around from generation to generation. That's the kind of mobility that a university degree is about for many (for most?) in the modern West.

The Corinthians knew something about that sort of mobility too. Among the cities of the ancient world, Corinth was unusual in the amount of social mobility that it had room for. Roman Corinth was a new city—in Paul's day, just a hundred years old. It was a colonial city, settled, for the most part, by freedmen, by ex-slaves. And it was a commercial city, a trading center, where fast, new money could be made. Aelius Aristides called it "the common emporium of Europe and Asia . . . the market . . . and festival of the Greeks."[4] If ever there was a city in the Roman empire where you could make money, climb the ladder, get ahead, and buy some status, Corinth was that city.

3. See further in chapter 7, below.

4. Aristides, *Discourses* 46.23.

And when Paul talks sarcastically about the Corinthian church in 1 Cor 4 as "already rich . . . already kings . . . wise . . . strong . . . held in honor," the implication is that the Christians in Corinth were just as concerned with climbing the ladder as their neighbors were. On issue after issue in the rest of the letter—attitudes to leaders, the toleration of sexual immorality, law suits, idol meat, temple feasts, the Lord's Supper, spiritual gifts—the problems of the Corinthian church can be traced back back, at least in part, to the fact that they are *misdirected*. Their hearts are set not on mission or on pilgrimage but on social acceptance and advancement.

Setting a direction: Paul's leadership in action

All this means that when Paul addresses those various problems, he doesn't just give a few instructions or remind them of a few rules or introduce a new programme. In the midst of all the mess and complexity, he sets a direction; he points them, by word and example, back to the goal they ought to be aiming at, and he shows them what it will look like for them to travel toward that destination. The remainder of this chapter will focus on one very particular example of how that works out, in 1 Cor 9–10, in relation to the issue of idol meat and idol feasts.

The Context: Idol meat and idol feasts

The context is the set of questions that arose in a pagan city like Corinth around the multiple connections between meat and feasting and idols. One of the principal ways in which you worshiped the gods of the ancient world was by sacrificing to them, which meant that the daily functioning of the temples involved an enormous slaughter of birds and animals. After the animals had been killed there was typically a feast of some sort in honor of the god, sometimes as a part of an official occasion like the Isthmian games, or as part of a gathering of a voluntary association like a trade guild or a funeral society. And then the remainder of the leftover meat was passed on to the butchers in the meat market to be sold along with any other meat that had been slaughtered that day.

All of this raised at least three questions for the Christians in the city. Now that they worshiped Jesus it would have been pretty obvious to most that they wouldn't be going off to the temple to initiate a sacrifice themselves. But what if they were invited to take part in the ritual meal afterward, at the temple, in honor of the god? What if they wanted to buy some meat at the market and there was no way of knowing whether it had or hadn't been originally slaughtered as a sacrifice to a god? Or what if they were just invited to dinner by a neighbor or a business associate, and their neighbor—or their neighbor's slave—was cooking the dinner?

Those were the kind of questions that arose for the Corinthians, and especially for the wealthier members of the congregation. They were the ones who had the money to afford meat as part of their regular diet; they were also the ones who had social and business connections that could be very helpfully advanced if they attended the dinner parties and ate at the various banquets and feasts in the temples of the city, and badly damaged if they didn't.[5]

Some of the Christians in the church, with hyper-sensitive consciences, were saying, "No, no, no!" to every one of those scenarios. Meat that had idol germs on it was not going to touch their lips under any circumstances. And others in the church, who were socially ambitious, eager to fit into the life of the city, and conscious of the sophistication of their ideas,[6] said things like, "all of us possess knowledge," and "no idol in the world really exists," and "there is no God but one," and "food will not bring us close to God," and "all things are lawful." They insisted on their right and their freedom to eat whatever they wanted, wherever they wanted, whenever they wanted.

Two imperatives

Paul responds to both groups—"the weak" and "the strong"—with a reminder of two imperatives that are aimed at redirecting their orientation and their aim.

(i) Mission (9:12–27)

In the first place, Paul reminds them of the imperative of mission. He's speaking in particular to the people who are fixated on their own rights and freedoms, and he reminds them about his own rights and freedoms as an apostle, and the way that he has been taught by Christ to use them.

5. See especially Theissen, *Social Setting*, 121–43; though note the criticisms and caveats argued for in Fotopoulos, *Food offered to Idols*, 12–15; and Cheung, *Idol Food*, 311–14.

6. See especially Brookins, "The Wise Corinthians."

> For though I am free with respect to all, I have made myself a slave to all, so that I might win more of them. To the Jews I became as a Jew, in order to win Jews. To those under the law I became as one under the law (though I myself am not under the law) so that I might win those under the law. To those outside the law I became as one outside the law (though I am not free from God's law but am under Christ's law) so that I might win those outside the law. To the weak I became weak, so that I might win the weak. I have become all things to all people, that I might by all means save some. I do it all for the sake of the gospel, so that I may share in its blessings. Do you not know that in a race the runners all compete, but only one receives the prize? Run in such a way that you may win it. Athletes exercise self-control in all things; they do it to receive a perishable wreath, but we an imperishable one. So I do not run aimlessly, nor do I box as though beating the air; but I punish my body and enslave it, so that after proclaiming to others I myself should not be disqualified. (9:19–27)

It is striking how conspicuously the life and the mindset that Paul describes here are depicted as heading somewhere, directed toward something. There is a *goal* that he has (verses 19–22) which he repeatedly describes as "winning people" and "saving" them. This is not just something that he does for his own sake, or even for theirs, but "for the sake of the gospel" (verse 23). That is to say, the goal that he pursues in proclaiming Christ and winning people to believe in him arises out of the *allegiance* that he has to the gospel of Christ, and to Christ himself whom the gospel proclaims. And yet this allegiance is not a disinterested allegiance. He doesn't serve Christ only because it is a good and noble and virtuous thing to do; he serves Christ not only out of duty but also out of *desire*—"I do it all for the sake of the gospel, so that I may share in its blessings."[7]

Those of us who have read a little too much Kant may want to clean Paul's motives up a little at this point, to make him say, "I do it all for the

---

7. Strictly speaking, the word "blessings" does not occur in the original Greek, and it is possible to translate the verse without making use of it at all, so that Paul is understood as saying something more like: "I do it all for the sake of the gospel, so that I may participate [fully] in its proclamation." (Cf. the argument for this reading in Thisleton, *First Corinthians*, 707.) But even if that reading is adopted, it still carries the implication that, as a *synkoinōnos*—a full participant, or shareholder—in the enterprise of the gospel, Paul would have looked forward to the prospect of sharing in its profits. The references in the following verses to the "prize" and "wreath" of the athlete, and Paul's desire not to be "disqualified", confirm (in a parallel pattern of imagery) the likelihood that verse 23 would have carried this implication.

sake of the gospel, so that others may share in its blessings," or "I do it all for the sake of the gospel, regardless of whether I end up sharing in its blessings." But it is we who are in error, not Paul, at this point. His deep, loyal allegiance to the cause of the gospel and his thirsty, passionate desire to share in its blessings are not competing drives but beautifully harmonious aspects of the one quest. He knows that it is gain, not loss, to serve the cause of Christ, so the sacrifices he describes are made willingly and gladly, without any sense of self-pitying virtuousness.[8]

The fruit of that goal, that allegiance, and that desire is a *resolve*. Paul describes the pattern of his life as a deliberate, determined, intentional use of the resources and the freedoms God has given him, in the cause of the gospel. That shows itself in two ways, which Paul describes on either side of the paragraph we have been examining.

In the first place (as Paul reminds the Corinthians in the preceding paragraphs) it shows itself in *sacrifice*.

> If others share this rightful claim on you, do not we still more? Nevertheless, we have not made use of this right, but we endure anything rather than put an obstacle in the way of the gospel of Christ. Do you not know that those who are employed in the temple service get their food from the temple, and those who serve at the altar share in what is sacrificed on the altar? In the same way, the Lord commanded that those who proclaim the gospel should get their living by the gospel. But I have made no use of any of these rights, nor am I writing this so that they may be applied in my case. Indeed, I would rather die than that—no one will deprive me of my ground for boasting! If I proclaim the gospel, this gives me no ground for boasting, for an obligation is laid on me, and woe to me if I do not proclaim the gospel! For if I do this of my own will, I have a reward; but if not of my own will, I am entrusted with a commission. What then is my reward? Just this: that in my proclamation I may make the gospel free of charge, so as not to make full use of my rights in the gospel. (9:12–18)

When Paul talks about becoming a Jew to the Jews and a Greek to the Greeks, he's not talking about a strategy of following the path of least resistance; he's not describing the lifestyle of someone who is desperate to fit in with the crowd around them so that they can be comfortable and accepted and popular. In the conversations that modern, Western Christians have about popular culture, fashion, music, food, and drink, it is all to easy for

---

8. See especially Piper, *Desiring God*, 239–52.

us to quote Paul's words from 1 Cor 9 as a legitimation for our own fearful, anxious desire to be accepted, fashionable, and esteemed. But that is not the spirit of what Paul is saying here. He's not talking about the adolescent fantasy of cool Christianity. He's talking about something much more adult than that, and much more Christ-like—about a costly, sacrificial willingness on his part to do the things that don't feel comfortable, to go to the places that he doesn't find it easy to go to, and to do it in the deliberate pursuit of the salvation of others. Paul is talking here about sacrifice, not syncretism.

And then secondly (according to the images in the paragraph that follows immediately after Paul's declarations in 9:19–23) the resolve of Paul to do all things for the sake of the gospel shows itself in a life of *discipline*: "Do you not know that in a race the runners all compete, but only one receives the prize? Run in such a way that you may win it. Athletes exercise self-control in all things; they do it to receive a perishable wreath, but we an imperishable one. So I do not run aimlessly, nor do I box as though beating the air; but I punish my body and enslave it, so that after proclaiming to others I myself should not be disqualified" (9:24–27).

The implication for us in Paul's example and exhortations is not a kind of Christian masochism, that finds pleasure or virtue in pain itself; the implication, rather, is a pattern of habitual, consistent, purposeful practices—things you do and things that you refrain from—as part of a deliberate ordering of your life toward the task of serving God and his mission. Paul's example suggests a pattern of life that will include intentional and disciplined habits of prayer, Bible reading, work, rest, self-denial, generosity, eating, drinking, abstaining, socializing, and of course the practice of evangelism itself—taking yourself to where people are who don't know Jesus and talking to them about him. That is the shape that Paul wants the Corinthians to see in his life, as a life directed toward the service of Christ and his gospel, and therefore as a life that involves resolve and sacrifice and discipline.

An influential twentieth-century echo of Paul's call in these verses can be found in the short pamphlet, *Sacrifice*, written in 1936 by Howard Guinness, the travelling Inter-Varsity Fellowship missionary who planted and nutured evangelical student groups in Canada, Australia, New Zealand, India, South Africa, Spain, Norway, Sweden, Finland, Hungary, Switzerland, and Belgium. Nearly eighty years on, the lifestyle of sacrifice and self-discipline that he urges on his readers comes across as something quaint, almost to the point of incomprehensibility. There are points, of course, at which this is simply a reflection of eight decades' worth of changes in language, technology, and social circumstances—a lifestyle driven by the same mind-set would end up looking very different in our own time.[9] But the changes of context run deeper than that; the strangeness and incomprehensibility we find in a text like *Sacrifice* are also, in no small part, a measure of the extent to which we are people who have been shaped by a culture of convenience and instant gratification. Self-denial and deferment of gratification are not skills in which we are well-trained, but they are essential disciplines for a life of mission.

(ii) Pilgrimage (10:1–22)

But the direction Paul wants the Corinthian church to remember is not only the outward-looking direction, *into* the world in mission, but also the forward-looking direction, *through* the world in holiness and pilgrimage. We see that most clearly in the following chapter, 1 Cor 10.

A STORY (10:1–11)

Paul begins by reminding the Corinthians of a story:

> I do not want you to be unaware, brothers and sisters, that our ancestors were all under the cloud, and all passed through the sea, and all were baptized into Moses in the cloud and in the sea, and all ate the same spiritual food, and all drank the same spiritual drink. For they drank from the spiritual rock that followed them, and the rock was Christ. Nevertheless, God was not pleased with most of them, and they were struck down in the wilderness. Now these things occurred as examples for us, so that we might not desire evil as they did. Do not become idolaters as some of them did; as it is written, "The people sat down to eat and drink, and they rose up to play." We must not indulge in sexual immorality as some of them did, and twenty-three thousand fell in a single day. We must not put Christ to the test, as some of them did, and were destroyed by serpents. And do not complain as some of them

9. In an insightful article ("Sacrifice: Have we given up?") written to mark the eighty year anniversary of Howard Guinness's arrival in Sydney, his successor at the Sydney University Evangelical Union, Rowan Kemp, reflects on what such a lifestyle might look like.

did, and were destroyed by the destroyer. These things happened to them to serve as an example, and they were written down to instruct us, on whom the ends of the ages have come. (10:1–11)

The story he reminds them of is not a randomly chosen one. It is the story of "our ancestors" (verse 1). The Corinthians are mostly Gentiles, not Jews, but they are Gentiles who have trusted in Christ and so have been grafted into the people of God. Spiritually they are the descendants of Israel, and this is their story—the story of "our ancestors." So Paul can say: "These things happened to them to serve as an example, and they were written down to instruct us, on whom the ends of the ages have come" (verse 11).

Paul reminds them of the story—the biblical story—that they belong to, and the point where they stand in that story. He wants them to see that the Israelites in the wilderness are a "type," an image or anticipation of them. Like the Israelites, they have experienced an act of divine deliverance and have set out on a journey. And like the Israelites they have not yet reached the destination. The promised land is still ahead of them, and there is still the danger that they might die in the desert. If they keep hankering after Egypt, worshiping the idols of the life they left behind, living the lifestyle of the pagan nations around them, then they will never inherit the land that God has promised them.[10]

A WARNING (10:11–22)

Coming out of that story in verses 1–11 is the warning in verses 11–22:

These things happened to them to serve as an example, and they were written down to instruct us, on whom the ends of the ages have come. So if you think you are standing, watch out that you do not fall. No testing has overtaken you that is not common to everyone. God is faithful, and he will not let you be tested beyond your strength, but with the testing he will also provide the way out so that you may be able to endure it. Therefore, my dear friends, flee from the worship of idols. I speak as to sensible people; judge for yourselves what I say. The cup of blessing that we bless, is it not a sharing in the blood of Christ? The bread that we break, is it not a sharing in the body of Christ? Because there is one bread, we who are many are one body, for we all partake of the one bread.

10. See especially Oropeza, "Echoes of Isaiah," 92–97; Hays, *The Conversion of the Imagination*, 8–12.

> Consider the people of Israel; are not those who eat the sacrifices partners in the altar? What do I imply then? That food sacrificed to idols is anything, or that an idol is anything? No, I imply that what pagans sacrifice, they sacrifice to demons and not to God. I do not want you to be partners with demons. You cannot drink the cup of the Lord and the cup of demons. You cannot partake of the table of the Lord and the table of demons. Or are we provoking the Lord to jealousy? Are we stronger than he?

Pastorally speaking the warning is beautifully constructed. Paul speaks to the Corinthians in their pride (verse 12), but also in their fear (verse 13). He appeals to their sense and their judgment (verse 15), and he invites them to reflect on the story of Israel, drawing rational conclusions about what it says about God and what it means to be in relationship with him. This is the kind of leadership, in other words, that addresses itself not only to the will but also to the intellect, the emotions, and the imagination. And it offers a direction—a direction, in this case, toward holiness of life, purity of devotion to God, and faithful perseverance in the pilgrimage of God's people, toward the goal of his Kingdom.

An overarching purpose: the glory of God (10:31—11:1)

Standing like a great arch over both the imperative to pilgrimage and holiness and the imperative to mission is a unifying vision of the glory of God. It is this great overarching commitment that explains why the two imperatives are not in competition with each other; the church that rightly understands how both holiness and mission relate to the glory of God is not torn between two competing directions but united in one quest.

The cause of God's glory is the ultimate reason for Paul's desire to win people and see them saved and to devote his life to the advance of the gospel; and the cause of God's glory is the ultimate reason why the holiness of his people and their perseverance in pilgrimage are so important. So Paul says (in 10:31–11:1): "whether you eat or drink, or whatever you do, do everything for the glory of God. Give no offense to Jews or to Greeks or to the church of God, just as I try to please everyone in everything I do, not seeking my own advantage, but that of many, so that they may be saved. Be imitators of me, as I am of Christ."

Direction-setting leadership

What does all this mean for the way we understand the task of leadership among God's people? The implication of what I've argued for in this chapter is this: if you are a leader then your job is to set a direction. To borrow a line from Stanley Hauerwas (who borrows it in turn from *Watership Down*), your job is "to say 'Let's do this,' and then live with the consequences."[11]

Usually this involves more than just popping up at the moment of decision and having the courage to propose a way forward; usually it involves an ongoing task that continues week in, week out, in between the big decisions. At the heart of that task is the work of keeping the story of Scripture vivid in people's memory and imagination, reminding them of its climax in the gospel, and drawing out the conclusions and implications that arise from it. Hand in hand with that, equally, it involves living a life yourself that points in the same direction as what you talk about. That is the way you set a direction and give a lead among the people of God, whether you're a Sunday school teacher or an archbishop or a pastor or a youth worker. The ingredients are much the same: courage; narrative; implications; example. And as I argued at the start of this chapter, because of the content of the gospel, there are two crucial dimensions that will always need to be present in the direction-giving leadership that we give to God's people.

Leading in holiness

Because the gospel points us forward to the coming Kingdom of God, reminding us that our allegiance is not to this world and that we do not worship its gods, leadership among God's people will always involve the job of leading in holiness. There will always be temptations and allurements—idolatries and immoralities like those Paul speaks of in 1 Cor 10—that threaten to tear people away from allegiance to Christ and prevent them from persevering toward the destination.

Leading in mission

And secondly, hand in hand with that, the task of a leader in God's church is not merely to point in the direction of holiness but also—at the same time—to point in the direction of mission. When Paul closes out this

11. Cf. Hauerwas, *A Community of Character*, 29.

section of the letter with his exhortation to the Corinthians to "be imitators of me, as I am of Christ," he has a specific context in mind, to do with idol meat and pagan temples. But the principle he gives is stated with the broadest of generality—"whether you eat or drink, or whatever you do"—and is directed toward the advantage and salvation of others, for the glory of God.

The two priorities—mission and holiness—are not competing ones, although there have been plenty of Christians over the centuries and in our own time who have acted as if they were, and have pitted the one against the other. The holiness we are called to is a holiness-in-mission, lived not in cloistered isolation from the world but in close proximity to those whom we are seeking to serve and evangelize. And the mission we are called to is a holy mission—one that has been entrusted to a people whose lifestyle is to stand out in sacred distinctiveness from the lifestyle of the surrounding world. It is within the same chapter, in the context of the same cluster of issues and decisions, and under the banner of the same quest to "do everything for the glory of God" (verse 32) that Paul tells the Corinthians both to "try to please everyone in everything" (verse 32) and to "flee from the worship of idols" (verse 14). Paul's injunction, "do not seek your own advantage, but that of the other" (verse 24, echoed in verse 33) applies as much to what he has said in the previous verses about holiness and concern for what will benefit and build up our fellow-believers (verse 23) as it does to what he goes on to say in the following verses about accepting dinner invitations and seeking the salvation of our non-Christian neighbors (verses 25–33).

Navigating a path through the complexities of social life that honors both of these imperatives can be a difficult and costly business. Good leadership provides both a clear reminder of the overall direction to which we have been called and a worked example of what it will look like in practice, in a particular context, to pursue that direction with ingenuity, integrity, and wisdom. It is to that theme of wisdom that we turn in the next chapter.

four

WISDOM

1 CORINTHIANS 1–2

Ader . . . the Idumæan; so long as he was in the land of Israel, and had not tasted the bread of the Egyptians, made no idols. It was when he fled from the wise Solomon, and went down into Egypt, as it were flying from the wisdom of God, and was made a kinsman of Pharaoh by marrying his wife's sister, and begetting a child, who was brought up with the children of Pharaoh, that he did this. Wherefore, although he did return to the land of Israel, he returned only to divide the people of God, and to make them say to the golden calf, "These be your gods, O Israel, which brought you up from the land of Egypt."[1]

Leadership and wisdom

Leadership is, among other things, an exercise of wisdom. If leading involves setting a direction, pointing a way forward, then doing that job well requires not only a clear sense of the big-picture vision that inspires the journey but also a careful attention to all the local and particular circumstances that require day-by-day, moment-by-moment decision-making along the way. Good navigation requires more than just correct and accurate reading of a correct and accurate map; it also requires a vigilant awareness of the

1. Origen, *Letter to Gregory*, 2.

various rocks and shoals, waves and currents through which the ship must travel, along with an understanding of the capacities and weaknesses of the ship, and the forces that must be harnessed to steer it safely through such waters. Good leadership, in other words, requires not only a worthy end but also a wise understanding of the ways and means required to achieve it.

The question of ways and means is not merely a pragmatic, technical, morally-neutral question; the landscape through which a path must be found is as much a moral and spiritual landscape as it is a material one. Thus, within 1 Corinthians, the example that Paul offers to his readers applies not only to the great end—"everything for the glory of God" (10:31)—that he pursues and commends to the Corinthians, but also and equally to the "ways" that he follows (4:17) in pursuing it. The exercise of leadership includes making decisions that are sometimes horrendously complicated, involving issues that are as much ethical as they are technical or tactical.

Nor should we think that the wisdom that is called for by the task of leadership is exercised only at the points of conscious decision-making. The wisdom that is required day by day, along the path, goes deeper than the conscious use of the intellect in solving problems and resolving dilemmas; as we saw in the previous chapter, it also involves the disciplined cultivation of habits and practices that embed it within the patterns and instincts of life. Wisdom has as much to do with shape and structures of life as it does to do with consciously-held, rationally-articulated worldviews and ideologies.

Wisdom is required too if you are to succeed in taking others with you toward that end, and persuading them to follow in wise and worthy ways along the journey. It is all very well for you to know the right destination yourself, and to travel in all the right paths toward it; but if no one else is travelling with you, then—whatever else you are—you are not a leader. According to Plato's parable in *The Republic*, the true philosopher (who would be the ideal king, if only the people were wise enough to ask him!) is profoundly uninterested in the arts of rhetoric and *Realpolitik*—he does not believe that there is "any art or science of seizing the helm, with or without the consent of others, or any possibility of mastering this alleged art and the practice of it at the same time with the science of navigation."[2] In other words, according to Plato, the ideal navigator is much too busy studying the stars and perusing the tide-charts to stoop to persuading others to let him take the helm. But even Plato, in his later works, finds some room for the art of rhetoric as a legitimate (and unavoidable) means of "lead[ing] the

2. *Republic*, 488d-e.

soul by means of words,"[3] and Aristotle his pupil built on that foundation a whole treatise on rhetoric, as an essential art for the communication and commendation of practical wisdom and its political implications. There is no way of bypassing the political and rhetorical dimensions of the wisdom that is involved in the exercise of leadership. Leaders who are naïve enough to think they are above all that usually end up either ineffectual or dangerous (or both!) in the leadership that they exercise.[4]

In more ways than one, then, leadership calls for wisdom—a wisdom that is nuanced and complicated and multifaceted, in keeping with the nature of the task. And it is on the theme of wisdom, including its political and rhetorical dimensions, that Paul focuses in the opening chapters of 1 Corinthians.

Wisdom, Politics and the Word of the Cross (1:10–31)

In the first chapter of the letter, it is the political dimensions of wisdom that are most evident in the appeal Paul makes to the Corinthians and the arguments that he marshals in support of it. This is evident from the very beginning of the letter body, which commences in 1:10 with the appeal that Paul makes to the Corinthians: "that all of you be in agreement and that there be no divisions among you, but that you be united in the same mind and the same purpose." As commentators going back to Joseph Lightfoot in the nineteenth century have noted, Paul's language in this verse is steeped in the idioms of ancient Greek politics.[5] Drawing together the threads of a comprehensive survey of the parallels between Paul's language in this verse and the language of the Greek polical tradition, Margaret Mitchell concludes: "1 Cor 1:10 is filled with terms which have a long history in speeches, political treatises and historical works dealing with political unity and factionalism."[6] Paul's appeal in verse 10 is a political appeal, couched in unmistakably political language.

3. *Phaedrus*, 261a.

4. In the introduction to a recent popular work on Christian leadership, Albert Mohler laments the prevalence of pastors and seminary students who are "driven by deep and passionate beliefs . . . heavily invested in knowledge, and . . . passionate about truth," but who "have never thought much about leadership, and are afraid that thinking too much about it will turn them into mere pragmatists." Mohler, *Conviction to Lead*, 19.

5. Cf. Lightfoot, *Notes*, 151 (where he cites instances from Thucydides, Aristotle and Polybius); and Mitchell, *Rhetoric of Reconciliation*, 68–80.

6. *Rhetoric of Reconciliation*, 79.

But the politics of Paul's appeal is not the politics of faction and self-promotion. Writing to a church that has been torn apart into rival factions (one of which says "I belong to Paul," either as its own slogan or as the slogan with which Paul impersonates its attitude) Paul does not simply go into battle for his own faction to shore up its prestige and power. Instead, he frames his appeal in terms of the politics of conviction and purpose: "that all of you be in agreement . . . united in the same mind and the same purpose."[7]

While Mitchell has amply demonstrated the extent to which Paul's language echoes the terminology of Greek political discourse, these parallels should not drown out the distinctively Christian content of the "mind" and "purpose" in which Paul hopes to see the Corinthians united. Concord and harmony are good things in themselves—"God is a God not of disorder but of peace" (14:33)—but Paul's concern is more particular than the generic preference for social harmony and order that he shared with the pagan political philosophers and orators. His appeal is "by the name of our Lord Jesus Christ," a name that has dominated the greetings and thanksgivings of the previous verses, which identify the Corinthian *ekklēsia* as one whose entire existence, purpose and allegiance are determined by their relationship to him. Read in context, Paul's desire that the Corinthians be "in agreement" (literally, "speaking the same thing") is not just a desire that they stop arguing, but a desire that they unite together in speaking the message that has been entrusted to them—the "testimony of Christ" to which Paul has already referred in verse 6.[8] And the "same mind" in which he

---

7. The expression that the NRSV translates here as "the same purpose" (Gk: *hē autē gnōmē*) can be used in political contexts to refer either to a common purpose, desire or intention (e.g., Isocrates, *Orations* 6.9) or to a shared opinion (e.g. Isocrates, *Orations* 6.37), the latter frequently supplying the grounds for the former. Here, the context, including Paul's own example which he goes on to point the Corinthians to in verse 17, supports the NRSV's decision to read *hē autē gnōmē* as indicating a shared purpose as well as the underlying conviction that gives rise to it. Cf. the depiction in Phil 1:5, 27 of the Philippians as "sharing" in the work of mission and "striving side by side with one mind for the faith of the gospel."

8. Note also the extended discussion of the message that "we speak" in 2:6–16. The primary reference of Paul's "we" in these verses is probably to himself and his fellow-workers, and the main role played by the Corinthians in these verses is not as fellow-speakers with Paul but as people who receive (or ought to receive) his testimony. But the shift from the singulars of 2:1–5 to the plurals of 2:6–16 does still widen the circle of those who can potentially be understood as being included among the speakers in the picture that Paul paints, and the characterization of the "we" in verse 12 as those who "have received not the spirit of the world, but the Spirit that is from God, so that we may

urges them to find agreement is not just any mind but the mind that he will go on in the following chapter to refer to as "the mind of Christ" (2:16).[9]

Paul is not the kind of "consensus politician" who keeps to the uncontroversial high ground, too frightened to declare a position on disputed matters; he gives ample evidence in the remainder of the letter that he is willing to take sides (e.g., 11:18–22) and alienate powerful opponents (e.g., 5:1–13), where that is needed to maintain the church's holiness and its fidelity to Christ. But the basic appeal that underlies all of his particular urgings and exhortations within the letter is to the core convictions and purposes that unite (or ought to unite) the whole Corinthian church, and that tie them together with "all those who in every place call on the name of our Lord Jesus Christ, both their Lord and ours" (1:2). This is not the easiest way of getting the political results that you are after. In the short term, it can be easier to win battles by the politics of faction and patronage—building up a power base of clients and admirers, cobbling together alliances with other factions through crafty deal-making, and targeting one's arguments at the prejudices and vested interests of particular sub-groups to win their support. In the long term, however, such politics is disastrous for the unity and holiness of the church (as it is for the health and integrity of any human community).[10]

Side by side with the language of "wisdom" in the opening chapter of 1 Corinthians is the language of "power," another reminder of the political context into which Paul's words about wisdom are directed. The language of "power" is first introduced in 1:17, when Paul reminds the Corinthians that "Christ did not send me to baptize but to proclaim the gospel, and not with eloquent wisdom, so that the cross of Christ might not be emptied

---

understand the gifts bestowed on us by God" has obvious resonances with the way Paul has described the Corinthians in the opening verses of the letter (1:5–7).

9. A similar train of thought can be found in Philippians 2, where Paul's appeal to the Philippians to be "of the same mind [*to auto phronēte*] . . . in full accord [*sympsychoi*] and of one mind [*to hen phronountes*] (2:2)" is given a very specific content by the narrative account that Paul goes on to offer of "the same mind [*touto phroneite*] . . . that was in Christ Jesus" (2:5) and its echoes in the attitude and conduct of Timothy and Epaphroditus (2:19–30).

10. There is of course a legitimate place for political compromises, and for alliances of convenience on particular issues, between individuals and communities who do not have the same core convictions and purposes. But these should only be the necessary expedients of particular situations, not the fundamental basis of the politics of a community—and certainly not of the community of the church.

of its power."[11] The close connection between the concepts of wisdom and power is continued in the following verse, where Paul contrasts the "foolishness" that those who are perishing find in the gospel with the "power" that it truly possesses, for those who are being saved (1:18), and it remains in view for the rest of the chapter: "Christ the power of God and the wisdom of God" (verse 24); "God's foolishness is wiser than human wisdom, and God's weakness is stronger than human strength" (verse 25); "not many of you were wise . . . not many were powerful" (verse 26); "God chose what is foolish in the world to shame the wise; God chose what is weak in the world to shame the strong" (verse 27).

What is at stake is a fundamental difference between the way that power works in the wisdom of the world and the way that it works in the wisdom of God. To dramatize that difference, in verse 19, Paul points the Corinthians back to the words that God speaks to the political leaders of Judah in Isa 29:14: "For it is written, 'I will destroy the wisdom of the wise, and the discernment of the discerning I will thwart.'" The original context of the Old Testament quotation is a situation in which the leaders of Judah are putting their trust in a military alliance with Egypt, to protect them from the threat posed by the rise of Assyria. Despite all the pious talk of the nation's leaders ("these people draw near with their mouths and honor me with their lips, while their hearts are far from me," says the immediately preceding verse in Isa 29) their "wisdom" in the end amounts to nothing more than a lurching progress from deal to deal, one calculation after another about which human power is the strongest one to seek protection from, and what undertakings must be given to secure that protection. The parallels with the Corinthians are not difficult to see:

> Isaiah's point is that God-talk is cheap and that God's action will shut the mouths of the wise talkers. Did Paul recall this full context when choosing an opening sermon text to chastise the Corinthians who were puffed up about their ability to speak in tongues and to speak about the things of God with eloquent rhetorical flourish? We may be reasonably sure that he did. The Corinthians, with their prized speech-gifts, make a show of possessing wisdom and honoring God with their lips, but their fractious behavior shows that in fact their hearts are far from God. Thus, like Judah in Isaiah's oracle, they stand under the sentence of divine judgment which

---

11. While the word "power" is not used in the Greek, the NRSV translators (along with those of most other English versions) are correct to take it as being implied by the context.

will nullify their professed wisdom and unmask their professed piety as a sham.[12]

If the political wisdom of the world is about finding the powerful ones and attaching oneself to them by deal-making and alliances, God's wisdom works according to an entirely different formula. Instead of seeking out the wise, the powerful and the people of noble birth, God seeks out "what is low and despised in the world, things that are not" as the objects of his election, and extends salvation to them through the "foolishness" of a gospel that proclaims a crucified Messiah. Paul spells out the logic and implications of this divine wisdom in verses 20–31:

> Where is the one who is wise? Where is the scribe? Where is the debater of this age? Has not God made foolish the wisdom of the world? For since, in the wisdom of God, the world did not know God through wisdom, God decided, through the foolishness of our proclamation, to save those who believe. For Jews demand signs and Greeks desire wisdom, but we proclaim Christ crucified, a stumbling block to Jews and foolishness to Gentiles, but to those who are the called, both Jews and Greeks, Christ the power of God and the wisdom of God. For God's foolishness is wiser than human wisdom, and God's weakness is stronger than human strength.
>
> Consider your own call, brothers and sisters: not many of you were wise by human standards, not many were powerful, not many were of noble birth. But God chose what is foolish in the world to shame the wise; God chose what is weak in the world to shame the strong; God chose what is low and despised in the world, things that are not, to reduce to nothing things that are, so that no one might boast in the presence of God. He is the source of your life in Christ Jesus, who became for us wisdom from God, and righteousness and sanctification and redemption, in order that, as it is written, 'Let the one who boasts, boast in the Lord.'

While the theological content of these paragraphs is rich and deep, it is not "pure" theology, devoid of any social context or implications. Paul reminds the Corinthians of these things at least partly in order to point out their implications for the way in which power is to be sought out and used in the politics of God's people. This much is clear, not only from the surrounding context of the letter, but also from the opening verses of the paragraph.

---

12. Hays, *First Corinthians*, 29.

There has been much discussion among the commentators about the precise intended reference of the terms that Paul uses for "the one who is wise" (*ho sophos*), "the scribe" (*ho grammateus*), and "the debater" (*ho syzētētēs*) in verse 20. The scope of Paul's language is intentionally broad—it is nothing less than the wisdom of "the world" (verse 20b) that he has in view.[13] But while the scope of Paul's sweeping rhetoric implies a broad applicability, to (all) the wisdom of (all) the world, its primary focus is still quite specifically concentrated on the way that wisdom functions as a source of *power*. The political context of the Isa 29 quotation and the emphasis on questions of power that runs parallel to the wisdom language in these paragraphs suggest that the figures Paul has in mind (the *sophos*, the *grammateus* and the *syzētētēs*) are selected principally because of the social prestige that they possess and the influence that they exert. One way or another, whether their particular spheres of expertise are bureaucratic, rhetorical, intellectual, or religious, they are all power-brokers, whose "wisdom" has a role to play in shaping what a community considers to be plausible, respectable, and expedient. And their wisdom, crucially, is the wisdom "of this age"—apocalyptic language for the present world order and its rulers, contrasted with the coming kingdom of God.[14] As Paul goes on to describe it in the following chapter, their wisdom is "a wisdom of . . . the rulers of this age, who are doomed to perish" (2:6).

Paul's account of how God has set himself against this brand of wisdom and shown it to be "foolishness" has far-reaching implications for how we are to understand and practice the politics of leadership among his people. The wisdom literature of the Old Testament provides a good precedent for learning from the distilled experience and technical expertise of the secular sages. As the people of God we are permitted—indeed encouraged—to plunder the Egyptians and use whatever gold they give to us for the worship and service of God.[15] But Paul's argument here in 1 Cor 1

13. There is no need, I think, to assume that Paul would have expected his readers to take *ho grammateus* as referring exclusively to the bureaucrats of the Greco-Roman world, or to read *ho sophos* as pointing only to the neo-sophistic orators of Paul's day. The close proximity to Paul's quotation from Isa 29:14 and the way in which Paul's questions echo the rhetoric of Isaiah in verses like Isa 19:12 and Isa 33:18 go against the view that the figures Paul has in mind are exclusively Greek, with no applicability to the "wise ones" of Jewish culture.

14. Technically the phrase "of this age" is attached only to the third figure, the debater, but the shape of Paul's larger argument strongly supports the assumption thay it is intended to reflect on all three.

15. Cf. Exod 3:19–22; 25:1–8 and the analogy with pagan wisdom in Origen, *Letter*

implies a sharp warning against any naïvety we may have about the extent to which that "secular" wisdom comes soaked in assumptions and habits of thought that are shaped by idolatrous narratives and practices. Secular wisdom is "secular" in the sense that it pertains to the tasks and structures of this age, but it is not "secular" in the sense of being value-free, or devoid of spiritual or religious content. Human beings and human cultures (including the post-Enlightenment cultures of the modern West as much as the Greco-Roman culture of the first century) are incorrigibly religious, and our views on what is rational, admirable, and wise are informed by deep-seated assumptions and desires that are reinforced daily by the habits and practices of life.[16] There are certainly lessons about leadership that can be learnt from the secular business and political sphere, just as there are lessons that can be learnt from the ants (Prov 6:6) and the birds (Matt 6:26), but in seeking to learn those lessons we must not forget that our measurements of what makes leadership "effective" and "successful" are relative to what we value and worship.[17]

> This, then, is the dark underbelly of the often-used analogy between Egyptian gold and secular wisdom. Secular wisdom, in the end, isn't just a collection of shapeless nuggets, or discrete techniques, that we can grab and bolt harmlessly on to our theology as we seek to serve God. Wordly wisdom affects our whole way of thinking, our way of relating, our way of speaking to one another. Corporate management textbooks invite us to speak (and

---

to Gregory, 2.

16. See especially Smith, *Desiring the Kingdom*, 17–130. Smith's particular focus is on those everyday habits and practices that count as "secular liturgies," where "liturgies" are defined as "rituals of ultimate concern: rituals that are formative for identity, that inculcate particular visions of the good life, and do so in a way that means to trump other ritual formations" (ibid., 86). As helpful as Smith's category of "secular liturgies" is in alerting us to the religious meaning and formative power of our habits and patterns of life, it is still best, I think, to view such activities as "liturgies" only by analogy. Many of them (e.g., shopping in the mall) have other functions that run parallel with or prior to their function as identity-forming rituals, and the meaning that they carry for particular individuals and in particular instances depends on the way that they combine with a whole matrix of other stories and practices. While Christians should be alert to the power of the secular city and its practices to shape their assumptions and desires, and deliberate about the way their habits of consumption shape and express their identity, there are some significant differences between a visit to the shops and a meal at the idol temple; it is possible to do the former as part of a life of worship offered up to God, but not (according to Paul's argument in 1 Cor 8–10) the latter.

17. Cf. Wells, "The D-Min-ization of the Ministry," 175–88.

therefore to think) about our church as a corporation. Music lessons encourage us to treat church as a performance. Self-help books invite us to believe that we can help ourselves. None of this is a reason to avoid secular wisdom altogether. In fact . . . we can't avoid using secular wisdom. But it does remind us that secular wisdom is inherently dangerous . . . One of the greatest challenges of Christian leadership is working out how to plunder the gold of the Egyptians without seeing a golden calf emerge from your ministry furnace.[18]

In the end, the way in which we practice the politics of leadership and the kind of wisdom that informs it will either harmonize or clash with the wisdom of God, and with his purpose to overthrow all vain, idolatrous and establish in its place a humble, joyful boasting "in the Lord" (1:31). A politics that trades on deals and alliances with the powerful, seeking out the wise, the influential, and the nobly-born, and placing its reliance on them, will inevitably find expression in a culture of exactly the kind of boasting that God is determined to destroy. A politics that places its trust in the message of the cross will be content—indeed delighted—to take its place among the "things that are not," and will make its boast (like Hannah in the Old Testament and Mary in the New) in the mercy and power of God.

Wisdom, Rhetoric and the Mind of Christ (2:1–16)

One obvious way in which this choice between two kinds of wisdom will play out is in the rhetoric that we use to influence and persuade others, and the way in which we evaluate the rhetoric of others. Rhetorical power is not the only kind of power that is at play in the politics of churches and other communities (there is also, for example, economic power, the power of technological expertise, and the power of social prestige and recognition), but in a voluntary community like the church where coercive physical force is rarely an option and leadership is largely by influence and persuasion, rhetoric is an indispensable weapon.

And 1 Corinthians is an unmistakably rhetorical letter. Paul is in the business of persuasion, and he wields words toward that end. As he puts it elsewhere in his correspondence with the Corinthians, "we destroy arguments and every proud obstacle raised up against the knowledge of God, and we take every thought captive to obey Christ" (2 Cor 10:4–5). But the

18. Windsor, "The Perils of Plundering the Egyptians."

kind of rhetoric that Paul employs is sharply different from what would have counted as skilful or sophisticated in the eyes of those who judged such things in first-century Corinth. Paul has already admitted as much in 1 Cor 1:17, when he reminds the Corinthians that "Christ did not send me to baptize but to proclaim the gospel, and not with eloquent wisdom, so that the cross of Christ might not be emptied of its power." Already in this verse, the implication is clear that the shape and style of Paul's rhetoric (". . . not with eloquent wisdom . . .") are not a mere accident or failure, or something trivial and incidental. They are a necessary outworking of what he was "sent" to do, and they serve a vital purpose: "so that the cross of Christ might not be emptied of its power."

In the opening verses of the following chapter, he returns to this theme, emphasizing once again that the rhetorical form of his preaching was tied inextricably to its content and purpose: "When I came to you, brothers and sisters, I did not come proclaiming the mystery of God to you in lofty words or wisdom. For I decided to know nothing among you except Jesus Christ, and him crucified. And I came to you in weakness and in fear and in much trembling. My speech and my proclamation were not with plausible words of wisdom, but with a demonstration of the Spirit and of power, so that your faith might rest not on human wisdom but on the power of God" (2:1–5).

The language Paul uses to describe the form that his rhetoric did not take makes it clear that he does not have in mind a wholesale rejection of all efforts to achieve clarity in communication or to use words as instruments of persuasion. What he is rejecting is "eloquent wisdom"; "lofty words or wisdom"; "plausible words of wisdom"—in other words, self-consciously elaborate rhetoric that seeks to win admiration for its own artistry, fancy rhetoric that flaunts the speaker's superior social status, and superficially plausible rhetoric that takes shortcuts to persuasion via the intellectual fashions of the day rather than seeking to lay bare the truth of the matter.[19] Rhetoric of this sort was in plentiful supply in first-century Corinth, and appears to have been greatly admired by some at least within the Corinthian church.[20] But Paul deliberately steers a course away from it, in favor of a mode of speech and conduct that drew attention not to his own eloquence or social superiority but to the substance of his message, which concerned the crucified Jesus and the power of God that raised him from the dead.

19. Cf. Pogoloff, *Logos and Sophia*, 131–32.
20. See especially Winter, *Philo and Paul among the Sophists*, 109–40.

Rhetoric always points somewhere, directing the attention of the listeners toward something that the speaker hopes will engage their understanding or their emotions. In Paul's case, he was determined that the effect of his preaching was not to point his hearers toward his own superiority as a speaker—to do so would be to pitch for converts whose faith "rest[ed] on human wisdom"—but to point his hearers toward "Jesus Christ, and him crucified."

The "weakness . . . fear, and . . . much trembling" in which Paul came to Corinth contrast sharply with the conventions that surrounded the initial visit to a city by an orator wanting to establish a reputation and a following.[21] The fact that he speaks of his "weakness" alongside his "fear and . . . trembling" offers support to the assumption of most commentators that he is referring, at least partly, to his anxieties and inadequacies in the face of his audience and his opposition on his first visit to Corinth.[22] But a likely additional resonance to his language derives from its background in the "fear and trembling" language of the Greek OT, suggesting that Paul may also have had in mind a reference to the fear of God, and its power to banish pretentiousness and conceit in preaching (cf. 2 Cor 4:2; 5:11).[23] If that is the case, then it stands alongside Paul's argument about the necessary correlation between the form of preaching and its cross-centered content to underline the extent to which his decisions about rhetorical strategy were shaped by deeply theological considerations. The sophistic fashions of first-century Corinth may have sharpened his resolve "to know nothing among you except Jesus Christ, and him crucified," so that he would not have been received as just another wisdom merchant, competing in the marketplace for admirers and adherents. But the bedrock of his reasoning transcends the particularities of the context. In any city, in any century, a decision to preach the gospel in a manner calculated to draw attention to the cleverness and rhetorical skill of the preacher amounts to a denial of the very message that is being preached; the same can be said of a church culture that idolizes skilful communicators as celebrities and puts its trust in their rhetorical power to draw a crowd and impress the hearers.

21. Cf. Aristides, *Discourses* 51; and Dio Chrysostom, *Discourses* 47, quoted in Winter, *Philo and Paul among the Sophists*, 144–48.

22. E.g., Fee, *First Corinthians*, 93–94; Witherington III, *Conflict and Community*, 123; Thiselton, *First Corinthians*, 215; cf. Acts 18:9–11.

23. Cf. Savage, *Power through Weakness*, 73.

In place of this misdirected trust and adulation, Paul urges a consistent focus on the message of the crucified Jesus and a humble reliance on the work of the Spirit: "nothing . . . except Jesus Christ, and him crucified . . . not with plausible words of wisdom, but with a demonstration of the Spirit and of power." Despite the fact that Paul's evangelism in Corinth was accompanied by "signs and wonders and mighty works" (2 Cor 12:1), most commentators agree that Paul is not talking here about the miracles that accompanied the message but about the power of the Spirit at work in the message itself.[24] Paul is not contrasting the power of miracles with the power of wisdom (as if he was happy to indulge the Jewish demand for signs but not the Greek demand for wisdom); rather, he is contrasting the power of God's spirit (at work in the message of the cross) with the power of mere rhetoric and human cleverness. A close parallel can be found in his description of the conversion of the Thessalonians, where he describes the gospel coming to the Thessalonians "not in word only, but also in power and in the Holy Spirit and with full conviction," a description that he fleshes out in terms of the deeply transformed lives of both the speakers and the hearers of the message—their boldness in the face of persecution, their joyful perseverance, and their turning from idols to the worship of God (1 Thess 1:5–10).

The kind of wisdom that Paul does preach, in reliance on the Spirit, is unpacked in the remainder of the chapter, where he makes it clear that his emphatic distinction between "the message of the cross" and "the wisdom of the world" is not intended to imply a wholesale rejection of wisdom, *per se*. The real conflict is not between the gospel and wisdom but between "the wisdom of this age" and "the wisdom of God" (revealed by the Spirit in the message of the gospel):

> Yet among the mature we do speak wisdom, though it is not a wisdom of this age or of the rulers of this age, who are doomed to perish. But we speak God's wisdom, secret and hidden, which God decreed before the ages for our glory. None of the rulers of this age understood this; for if they had, they would not have crucified the Lord of glory. But, as it is written, "What no eye has seen, nor ear heard, nor the human heart conceived, what God has prepared for those who love him"—these things God has revealed to us through the Spirit; for the Spirit searches everything, even the depths of God. For what human being knows what is truly human except the human spirit that is within? So also no one comprehends what

24. E.g., Fee, *First Corinthians*, 95; Garland, *1 Corinthians*, 87.

is truly God's except the Spirit of God. Now we have received not the spirit of the world, but the Spirit that is from God, so that we may understand the gifts bestowed on us by God. And we speak of these things in words not taught by human wisdom but taught by the Spirit, interpreting spiritual things to those who are spiritual. Those who are unspiritual do not receive the gifts of God's Spirit, for they are foolishness to them, and they are unable to understand them because they are spiritually discerned. Those who are spiritual discern all things, and they are themselves subject to no one else's scrutiny. "For who has known the mind of the Lord so as to instruct him?" But we have the mind of Christ.

The "secret and hidden" wisdom Paul speaks of here, as something that he communicates "among the mature," should not be understood as something elitist, arcane or esoteric. It is a mystery that "God has revealed to us through the Spirit." And the "mature" and "spiritual" ones among whom it is spoken and understood are not a privileged subset of the Christian community—however much the usage of such terms among the Corinthians would have implied that—but all those who have received the spirit of God (verse 12).

The content of this wisdom revealed by the Spirit is not something new and different from what Paul has already been talking about in the preceding paragraphs. Paul's assertion that the rulers of this age, if they had understood this wisdom, "would not have crucified the Lord of glory," and the way in which he sums up his claims in the paragraph's bottom line— "but we have the mind of Christ"—combine to suggest that the "wisdom" Paul has in mind here is neither more nor less than the message of the cross. That message is, after all, the message that he has already described in the previous chapter as "the power (and, by implication, the wisdom) of God" (1:18). It is *this* wisdom—which is also, at the same time, a kind of anti-wisdom—that gives a distinctively Christian shape and content to faithful Christian leadership.

To say this is not to sweep away the need for deep thought and creative improvisation, to dismiss the quest for coherence and understanding, or to despise the value of accumulated experience and lived example. The fact that "the Lord will give you understanding in all things" does not eliminate the need to "think over what I say" (2 Tim 2:7). And the fact that the "mind . . . that was in Christ Jesus" was perfectly exemplified in his incarnation and journey to the cross does not do away with the usefulness of the close, visible, lived examples of what it might look like to think with that mind and imitate that journey in new and different circumstances (Phil 2:5; 3:15–17). In other words, there is such a thing as a Christian *wisdom*, and it is essential for the task of leadership among God's people. But Paul's point in 1 Cor 1–2 is that it must genuinely be a *Christian* wisdom—a wisdom that thinks and speaks and acts with fear and trembling before God, that boasts not in itself but in him, and that generates patterns of speech and life that fit with the message of the crucified Jesus.

Christian leadership is not an ethereal, otherworldly practice, that floats above the earth in saintly but naïve impracticality. Nor is it simply a matter of abstract, intelligent, doctrinal correctness, detached from the realities and complexities of life on the ground. As a form of wisdom, it deals with (among other things) the politics of how power is gained and used among God's people and in the world, and it exercises a deliberate, purposeful rhetoric directed toward the persuasion of others. But its politics and its rhetoric is not an uncritical mimicry of the politics and rhetoric of the world; instead, it is a politics and a rhetoric shaped by the message of the cross, seeking with humility and integrity to unite God's people in the mind of Christ and apply that mind to the decisions and dilemmas of life. Leadership among God's people that operates with a different aim or a different strategy may be a wisdom of one sort or another, but it is not a *Christian* wisdom, and the kind of community that it fosters will not be a Christian community.

five

TRADITION

1 CORINTHIANS 11:17–26; 15:1–11

> What I am therefore is in key part what I inherit, a specific past
> that is present to some degree in my present. I find myself part of
> a history and . . . whether I like it or not, whether I recognize it or
> not, one of the bearers of a tradition.[1]

> Happy are those who concern themselves with these things, and
> those who lay them to heart will become wise. (Sir 50:28)

The modernist myth

IN THIS CHAPTER WE turn from the intuitive to the counter-intuitive; from
what seems obvious to us—that leadership is about setting a direction and
wisely pursuing it—to what may seem far less obvious to many of us: that
leadership involves receiving an inheritance and following in a tradition.
Leadership, the textbooks tell us, is about vision, goals, strategy, innova-
tion—in other words, the future—whereas tradition is about the past, and
can therefore be safely ignored. There are many reasons why this connection between leadership and tradition may seem less than obvious to us but

---

1. Macintyre, *After Virtue*, 221.

a crucial contributing factor is the influence that the central narrative of modernism has on the way we (Christians included) think about leadership.

One way to crystallize the difference that modernism makes to the way we see leadership is to think for a moment about a point of ambiguity that was left unexamined in the metaphor that I invoked in the introduction to this book. In the introductory chapter, I offered the suggestion that leadership is, in part, a direction-giving function. The implication, as I argued in chapter 3, was that a group that requires leaders is a mobile community—a community that is (or ought to be) going somewhere. Sometimes, of course, that is literally the case—a leader is taking people on a journey through space, from Egypt to Canaan, or from Troy to Ithaca, or from Spain to the New World. But more often the journey is a metaphorical one, from the situation of the present to some new state of affairs in the future.

If you're a modernist, then the future that we're traveling toward is a place that doesn't exist yet, because it's a place that we intend to build for ourselves. For the modernist, a leader is a pioneer, boldly going where no one has gone before. Your back is to the past, your face is to the future, and the people of the past can largely be ignored—the past is what you're climbing out of, and that is where your predecessors belong. That is the basic posture of modernism. But if you're a premodern person, that isn't necessarily the case. You're on a journey, and the people of the past aren't just behind your back; there's also a sense in which they are ahead of you, as the people who've gone before you, in whose footsteps you are following.

When you stop and think about it for a second or two, neither of those perspectives is literally true. The people of the past are not literally in front of us or behind us; time ("past" and "present") and space ("behind" and "in front") are different dimensions altogether. But both metaphors have some truth to them. There is a partial truth in the modern perspective; for us, indeed, the future is a place we've not yet visited, inhabited by people not yet born. But there is a partial truth too in the premodern perspective; many of the experiences we await in the as-yet-unknown future are experiences that our predecessors have undergone before us—serving within the same communities, sailing on the same ocean, laboring undering the same sun, being buried in the same soil.

There is, therefore, an inescapable connection between leadership and tradition. The connection is not necessarily one of slavish repetition—our interaction with tradition needs to be a critical interaction, and there are some customs that (as Hamlet put it) are more honored in the breach than the observance. But even when we are repudiating a tradition or reshaping it, we are still interacting with it; we are never writing on a completely blank sheet of paper. Leadership always involves an engagement of some sort with tradition—with the inheritance, good and bad, that you receive from those who have gone before you.

Gospel tradition

If we are leaders within the people of God, then the core tradition that we receive and pass on is the gospel. We didn't make it up; we didn't discover it; we received it. In the case of almost all of us—barring angelic appearances, night visions and divine visitations—we received it through some form of human transmission, within the community of the church. As gospel people, our attitude toward tradition in general needs to be determined by our attitude toward *gospel* tradition in particular. In this chapter, therefore, we will focus on two key passages in 1 Corinthians in which Paul speaks to the church in Corinth about the gospel traditions he received and passed on to them, and models for us a faithful interaction with the traditions that are developed and handed on among God's people.

"I received from the Lord . . ."

The first passage is in 1 Cor 11, and it begins with an example of a corrupted tradition—Paul is dealing with a practice that has evolved away from the meaning it originally had and was meant to have, and needs to be either restored or eradicated. At the start of the chapter, Paul has commended the Corinthians for "maintain[ing] the traditions just as I handed them on to you" (verse 2), before offering them a clarification of the meaning and rationale of the traditions regarding gender and head coverings within the gathering of the church. Now, however, in verse 17, he turns to a practice in which he can offer no such commendation.

Corrupted tradition (11:17–22)

> Now in the following instructions I do not commend you, because when you come together it is not for the better but for the worse. For, to begin with, when you come together as a church, I hear

that there are divisions among you; and to some extent I believe it. Indeed, there have to be factions among you, for only so will it become clear who among you are genuine. When you come together, it is not really to eat the Lord's supper. For when the time comes to eat, each of you goes ahead with your own supper, and one goes hungry and another becomes drunk. What! Do you not have homes to eat and drink in? Or do you show contempt for the church of God and humiliate those who have nothing? What should I say to you? Should I commend you? In this matter I do not commend you! (11:17–22)

The custom Paul is speaking about here is that of the Corinthians' community meal. The meal, it seems, was an integral part of what the Corinthians did when they gathered: they gathered to eat and drink as a people who belonged together, and who belonged together to Jesus. But Paul tells the Corinthians that the way they are conducting the meal suggests that they are not celebrating it as "the Lord's Supper" at all; they are celebrating it as if it were their own private dinner party. The wealthy Corinthians (sitting apart, perhaps, in the superior accommodation of the *triclinium*)[2] would eat and drink to their hearts' content, and the poorer members of the congregation—"those who have nothing"—would be left to go hungry. The whole thing had the effect of reinforcing the status of the special few and humiliating the rest.[3]

The true story (11:23–26)

In response to that Corinthian custom—that corrupted tradition that has come to function "not for the better but for the worse"—Paul reminds them of what the meal ought to have meant. It is impossible to say with certainty whether the custom of the meal was something the Corinthians themselves had initiated, as a Christian equivalent to the meals that the pagans ate in honor of their gods, or whether the meal itself was part of what Paul received from Jesus and the first disciples and passed on to them—a direct continuation of that pattern in the Gospels in which Jesus ate and drank with his disciples and kept table fellowship with sinners. Most probably, given the language that Jesus uses about a repeated meal and a repeated remembrance, the meal itself is part of what Paul taught the Corinthians to

2. Cf. Thiselton, *First Corinthians*, 859–62.
3. See especially Winter, *After Paul Left Corinth*, 142–51.

do, and the story of the Last Supper went hand in hand with the practice of the Lord's Supper from the beginning. But either way, Paul tells us that the story about Jesus' last meal with his disciples and the things that he said at that meal was something that was passed on to Paul, and something that he in turn passed on to the Corinthians.

> For I received from the Lord what I also handed on to you, that the Lord Jesus on the night when he was betrayed took a loaf of bread, and when he had given thanks, he broke it and said, "This is my body that is for you. Do this in remembrance of me." In the same way he took the cup also, after supper, saying, "This cup is the new covenant in my blood. Do this, as often as you drink it, in remembrance of me." For as often as you eat this bread and drink the cup, you proclaim the Lord's death until he comes. (11:23–26)

The story Paul passed on to the Corinthians is not something that is arbitrarily pasted onto the community meal as a dispensable liturgical extra. Paul wants the Corinthians to know (verse 26) that the function of the very meal itself ought to be to say something about the death of Jesus. He tells them the true story (verses 23–25) and he underlines for them what the point of it is: to "proclaim the Lord's death."

Telling the story truly (11:27–34)

In the paragraph that follows, he spells out what it will mean for them to tell that story *truly* in what they do.

> Whoever, therefore, eats the bread or drinks the cup of the Lord in an unworthy manner will be answerable for the body and blood of the Lord. Examine yourselves, and only then eat of the bread and drink of the cup. For all who eat and drink without discerning the body, eat and drink judgment against themselves. For this reason many of you are weak and ill, and some have died. But if we judged ourselves, we would not be judged. But when we are judged by the Lord, we are disciplined so that we may not be condemned along with the world. So then, my brothers and sisters, when you come together to eat, wait for one another. If you are hungry, eat at home, so that when you come together, it will not be for your condemnation. About the other things I will give instructions when I come. (11:27–34)

For the purposes of the issue that we are focusing on in this chapter, the point here is not the details, important as they are. The point here, for our purposes, is what Paul is doing as a leader who has received the story of Jesus and passed it on to the Corinthians. There's more than that going on, of course. Paul is writing as an apostle, not just as a pastor; as an apostle he is doing for the Corinthians something more closely analogous to what the Scripture does for us. But hand in hand with that—at the level we're focusing on in this chapter—he is modeling for us what we too are to do as leaders. He is acting as a leader who has received the story of Jesus and passed it on to the Corinthians, along with patterns and practices that go with it, and who is determined to keep urging and assisting the Corinthians to perform the meal and tell the story faithfully, fittingly, worthily.

That is, most likely, what Paul means means by not "eating the bread and drinking the cup in an unworthy manner." He has already told the Corinthians in verse 26 that "eating the bread and drinking the cup" is meant to be a proclamation of Jesus' death. The way the meal is to do that is not only in the accompanying liturgy that gets recited in words but in the conduct of the gathering and what it says in actions. The whole manner in which they perform the meal is meant to show the imprint of Jesus the suffering servant, the one who did not seek his own advantage but poured out his life for others. If the way in which they conduct the meal fails to discern the body of Christ (as Paul puts it in verse 29)—that is to say, if the way in which they conduct the meal fails to show that they are honoring the people at the table with them as fellow members of Christ's body—then the very thing that they are doing as they gather is part of the self-glorifying arrogance on which the cross announces God's judgment. They are eating and drinking judgment on themselves. Telling the story truly involves "examin[ing] yourselves," "discerning the body," and "waiting for [or perhaps, better, 're-ceiving,' i.e. honoring and extending hospitality to] one another."[4]

Gospel tradition is a complicated thing. Barring a miracle like the Damascus road or the appearance of an angel from heaven, the only way you and I are going to receive the gospel is as it's passed down through human hands. Each generation of the church receives the gospel from those who had it before them. We are always inheritors; we should always be thankful, and honor our fathers and mothers in Christ. There is something

4. Cf. Winter, *After Paul left Corinth*, 151–55. Winter argues convincingly that the verb translated in the NRSV as "goes ahead with" should better be translated as simply "devours," without any necessary implication that the richer members of the congregation were eating and drinking their private meal before the poorer members arrived.

inexcusably childish about a form of Christianity that has not yet learnt these basic lessons of receptivity, thankfulness, and honor. But it is also the task of the church in each new generation—and the task of its leaders especially—to critically examine what has been done with that inheritance. Honoring the preciousness of the gospel requires us not only to be thankful to those who passed it down to us, but also to ask whether there are customs that have evolved during the process of transmission that are not worthy of that gospel. Where necessary, the preciousness of the gospel requires us to go to war with the corruptions in the tradition, for the sake of the meaning that is at its core.

"I handed on to you as of first importance . . ."

Contagious unbelief (15:12, 33–34)[5]

But it's not just corrupted tradition—the distortions that we inherit from the church of yesterday and the customs that evolve amongst the church of today—that endangers the faithful preservation and transmission of the gospel. It's also the contagious unbelief of our neighbors around us, inside and outside the church. The church in any generation always exists on two axes: a longitudinal axis, in which the church exists between the church of yesterday and the church of tomorrow, and a latitudinal axis, in which the church relates within the world of the present to the people of the sur-rounding society. All the way through 1 Corinthians Paul keeps on coming back to the topic of how the Corinthian church relates to the city around it, how the believers in Corinth relate to the neighbors amongst whom they live.

And it's complicated, as we saw briefly in chapter 3, above. Paul doesn't want the Corinthian Christians to disengage from their city and their neighbors. He doesn't want them to leave the world, to stop accepting the dinner party invitations, to shun the sexually immoral and the greedy and idolators and the revilers and the drunkards (cf. 5:9–13; 10:27–30). The kind of holiness he wants to call them to is a holiness-in-mission. But he's not naïve about the pressures that this calling places on them, and the pos-sibility that their neighbors will influence them more than they influence their neighbors.

---

5. These verses and ideas are also touched on in chapter 7, below.

The heart of it all has to do with belief in the resurrection. The Corinthian church is meant to be the kind of community that believes God raises the dead. And their neighbors do not believe that. They're not all skeptics and Epicureans; many of them believe in some sort of afterlife, hopefully a blessed one. But the idea of the resurrection of corpses was almost universally regarded as irrational and distateful. And the notion that you would bet your life on it—that you would pour your whole life out in the service of Christ, giving and suffering and risking in the hope of being raised again one day—that notion would have been completely foreign to the culture of the city.[6] So when Paul says in verse 12 that there are some among the Corinthians who say there is no resurrection of the dead, the source of that belief seems to be at least in part the influence of the social context that they live in. All around them is a city built on the assumption that it is the accumulation of present power and present pleasure and present honor that is the great goal of life, and scoffs at the idea of something sure and certain and bodily on the other side of the grave.[7]

Once again, as in chapter 11, there is a pattern of life that goes with believing the gospel, and a contrasting pattern of life that goes with denying it, and the Corinthians are in danger of being sucked by the pressures of social conformity into a belief system and a lifestyle that accommodates to the world around them. Belief and unbelief are socially transmitted dispositions; they are not just internal, existential experiences or theoretical, intellectual opinions. You believe or disbelieve as a person who influences and is influenced in a social situation. How you act and how you relate to the people around you are inseparably connected with what you believe, and the influences between intellectual belief and social behavior run in both directions. So Paul says (verses 32–33): "If the dead are not raised, 'Let us eat and drink, for tomorrow we die.' Do not be deceived: 'Bad company ruins good morals.'"

6. See especially Wright, *Resurrection*, 81–84; 315–16.

7. See Witherington III, *Conflict and Community*, 295–98, for a helpful summary of some of the ways in which this set of pagan beliefs and aspirations was drawn upon and reinforced by the Roman imperial propaganda that was so prominent in the culture of the city.

The core message (15:1–11)

In response to that contagious unbelief that is white-anting the Corinthians' faith, Paul reminds them of the core message that he passed on to them at the beginning, when they first believed:

> Now I would remind you, brothers and sisters, of the good news that I proclaimed to you, which you in turn received, in which also you stand, through which also you are being saved, if you hold firmly to the message that I proclaimed to you—unless you have come to believe in vain. For I handed on to you as of first importance what I in turn had received: that Christ died for our sins in accordance with the scriptures, and that he was buried, and that he was raised on the third day in accordance with the scriptures, and that he appeared to Cephas, then to the twelve. Then he appeared to more than five hundred brothers and sisters at one time, most of whom are still alive, though some have died. Then he appeared to James, then to all the apostles. Last of all, as to one untimely born, he appeared also to me. For I am the least of the apostles, unfit to be called an apostle, because I persecuted the church of God. But by the grace of God I am what I am, and his grace toward me has not been in vain. On the contrary, I worked harder than any of them—though it was not I, but the grace of God that is with me. Whether then it was I or they, so we proclaim and so you have come to believe. (1 Cor 15:1–11)

The gospel, for Paul, is not just a door that you walk through at the start of the Christian life, but a rock that you stand on for the rest of your days. It is a gospel you need to be to be reminded of; it is a gospel in which you (continue to) "stand"; it is a gospel through which you "are being" saved.

Those of us who are called to serve as leaders, teachers, and preachers among God's people must therefore never be embarrassed of preaching to the choir, evangelizing the church, reminding God's people of the gospel that they depend upon every day. We are not *just* to do that—we are also called to take the gospel to those who haven't yet heard and don't yet believe it. But a fundamental part of our job is to do what Paul is doing here—evangelizing God's people with the gospel they already know. The same applies to the work of a Bible study leader or a youth pastor or a father or a mother or a theology lecturer; in fact, the same applies to the way in which we speak inwardly to ourselves as well, reminding ourselves day by day of the gospel we have believed in.

Here, in verses 1–11, Paul reminds the Corinthians of the core content of the gospel that he received and passed on to them. In the first place (verse 3) he reminds them that the gospel contains the message that "Christ died for our sins." The language is that of Isa 53: "He was wounded for our transgressions; he was crushed for our iniquities; upon him was the chastisement that brought us peace, and with his stripes we are healed." It's the language of substitution—that he stood in our place; that he suffered the penalty of death that we deserved. Christ died for our sins.

Secondly, Paul writes: "Christ died for our sins *in accordance with the scriptures.*" The Scriptures that Paul has in mind are the Scriptures of the Old Testament, the Scriptures of Israel that promised and foreshadowed the death of a suffering Messiah, and provided the whole enormous narrative framework within which Paul understood the story of Christ. For Paul, it matters, and it is fundamental to the gospel, that the Christ who saves is not some Christ that we imagine for ourselves but the Christ of Scripture and history—the Christ who was promised by the prophets and testified to by the apostles.

If we see the essence of our task as being an attempt to market Christianity in a post-Christian world, the temptation will always be there for us to reinvent the product to make it more appealing. Back in the earliest days of Christianity, when the gospel message first went out to the Gentiles, the temptation was already there to reinvent Jesus as just another Gentile divinity, as the patron of a new Greek mystery religion. The temptation was there to cut the links between the Christ of faith and the Jesus of history—the Jewish Jesus, the Jesus whose mission and message and identity were grounded in the Scriptures of the Old Testament. It would have made sense; it would have made things so much easier. And in our own day too the temptation is there to tone down Jesus, to make him less confronting, less absolutist, less counter-cultural. The temptation is there to pull the gospel message out of its biblical context, in which it is announced and narrated as the climax of the big biblical story about God and Israel (which is itself part of the still larger biblical story about creation, blessing, sin, accountability, judgment, and resurrection) and insert it into some other narrative about self-improvement or personal prosperity or social reform. But Paul insists that the gospel he preaches is a gospel "in accordance with the scriptures."

Paul's summary continues: "he was buried." Paul includes the burial here in this gospel summary presumably because it shows that Christ's death was a physical death, and his resurrection was a bodily resurrection.

What ever happened between Friday night and Sunday morning, it involved the physical body of Jesus that was crucified outside Jerusalem and placed in the borrowed tomb of Joseph of Arimathea. As the Apostles' Creed says, "he was crucified, dead, and buried."

And "he was raised." He was raised on the third day—again, "in accordance with the Scriptures." The resurrection of Jesus is the point that Paul goes on to emphasize across the rest of this chapter. He emphasizes it not because he thinks the Corinthians don't believe it—he knows that they do, at least in theory. He emphasizes it not because they don't believe it but because they don't see how important, how foundational it is; because they are not living and thinking in the light of it.

These things are not the inventions of a visionary genius; they are the givens of basic Christianity, the inheritance we receive, the foundation we stand on. The humbling implication for those of us who serve as Christian leaders is that the things "of first importance" in our ministry are not the visionary dreams or the clever strategies that we contribute but the core traditions that we have received and been charged with handing on.

Morning-after ministry (15:33–34, 58)[8]

This does not mean that Christian leadership is simply a matter of comfortable, steady-as-she-goes continuation of the way things have been, or easy, incremental improvement. Here in chapter 15, as was the case in chapter 11, the reminders that Paul gives to the Corinthians are brought into sharp collision with the present practices of a church that has fallen under the spell of the culture in which they live. Having reminded the Corinthians of the gospel—the core traditions that he received and passed on to them— and having reasoned with them (verses 12–32) about the inconsistency between saying they believe that gospel and speaking, thinking, and living as if there was no future resurrection for God's people, Paul turns to them in verses 33–34 and says: "Do not be deceived: 'Bad company ruins good morals.' Come to a sober and right mind, and sin no more; for some people have no knowledge of God. I say this to your shame."

Paul's ministry with the Corinthians is often—as it is here—a kind of morning-after ministry. He tells them the gospel and he sets them on the path of following Christ, and then they go out on the town on Saturday night and he arrives next morning to find them crashed on the lounge and

---

8. These verses and ideas are also touched on in chapter 7, below.

smelling like a distillery. Again. So he puts them in the shower and makes them a coffee and sits down with them and he tells them the gospel again, and he warns them about what will happen if this continues. There is love in his words, but there's a fair bit of sternness too, for their sake and for the sake of the honor of Jesus. So here he not only reminds them (verses 1–11) but he also warns them (verses 33–34) and he urges them (verse 58) not to give up: "Therefore, my beloved, be steadfast, immovable, always excelling in the work of the Lord, because you know that in the Lord your labor is not in vain."

Leadership that faithfully ministers the gospel tradition does not take place within an imaginary church of ecclesiastical nostalgia, safely sheltered from the seductions and distractions of the present age. It ministers the gospel within the real—and therefore frequently frustrating and disappointing—church of the present, with the patient kindness and urgent confrontation that the gospel itself demands.

Leaders are followers

If leadership for us is defined in the light of the gospel, and if the gospel is the core tradition of the community in which we lead, then leadership has an irreducible element of traditioning. Leaders are followers—followers of the Lord Jesus, and followers in the footsteps of those who served him before us and passed on the gospel to us. We lead with gratitude, as people who have received a precious gift, and with a humble appreciation of those who have passed it on to us. And we lead as people who are charged with the responsibility of receiving that gift well, and passing it on to the people coming after us, helping God's people to keep telling the story, and to keep telling it truly.

Local forebears

What counts as "tradition" will mean different things in different contexts, as will the dynamics of how traditions are created, received, and handed on. The reality is, even in a group as transient as as an independent church plant or a university student ministry, there are forebears who passed the gospel on to you and who shaped the traditions that you have inherited. A group does not exist simply within the moment in time that is the present. Its existence sprawls across the months and years and decades and centuries.

An important part of the work of a leader is to examine the various customs and practices that have evolved within the history of the group, and to discern which of them are wise and faithful responses to changing circumstances and which of them—like the Corinthian meals—are aberrations from the gospel and need to be hauled back to where they ought to be.

Gospel forebears

Behind the local forebears of the last century or so in the church or group or denomination that you or I belong to are the long lines of gospel forebears, who passed the word of the gospel down to us across the generations—those who took it to new places and those others who kept its memory alive within the places from which they went; those who fought for its integrity and those, at times, who distorted its meaning and lost its centrality.

The traditioning church does not have authority over the traditioned gospel. Rather, as Paul insists here in 1 Corinthians, it is the gospel—the prophetic and apostolic testimony to the saving work of God in Jesus—that is the criterion against which the performance of the church in any generation is to be evaluated. The story that matters is not the story of an evolving church, adapting its message to fit with its changing times; it is the story of the mighty works of God in Christ, their proclamation to the ends of the earth, and their transmission from one generation to the next. You and I are part of that story, and the leadership we exercise in our time will be part of the process by which the gospel is handed down to the people who come after us.

Faithful traditioning

This means that a crucial part of your leadership and mine in this generation of the churches and groups in which we serve will be the faithful traditioning of the gospel. If we understand the story we are part of, we will remember those who went before us, and appreciate and honor them as our fathers and mothers in Christ, and we will be prepared to critique the customs and the formulations that we received from them, along with the ones that we have developed in our own time too. We are, in Paul's words, to "examine ourselves" (collectively as well as individually) to make sure that we continue to proclaim Christ worthily and fittingly in our words and our practices.

And our responsibility does not stop with the present. Our responsibility to broadcast the gospel along the "latitudinal" axis to the people of the world today among whom we live co-exists with a second responsibility to preserve and hand on the gospel along the "longitudinal" axis to the church of tomorrow. The story of God's salvation must be told both outwards, to "the ends of the earth," and onwards, to "a people yet unborn" (Ps 22:27, 31). The moment of our present existence as the church sits perched between the past from which we inherited the gospel and the future to which we will bequeath it. That gives us a solemn responsibility to make preparations for those who will come after us—to teach our children and our children's children, to train the successors who will follow in our footsteps and multiply the gospel, and to guard the good deposit of the message against the incremental aberrations that could be dangerous in our own time and deadly in our grandchildren's. In all of these things, we are called to do our part in ensuring that the message of the gospel continues to believed and taught and loved and proclaimed, not just as a footnote or a formality but as the integrating center to all of the church's thinking and saying and doing.

six

EDIFICATION

1 CORINTHIANS 3:1–16; 14:1–40

We cannot do everything,
And there is a sense of liberation in realizing that.
This enables us to do something, and to do it very well. . . .
We may never see the end results,
But that is the difference
Between the master builder and the worker.
We are workers, not master builders,
Ministers, not messiahs.
We are prophets of a future that is not our own.[1]

Leaders are builders

In all the previous chapters of this book (as is the case in those that follow) the dominant metaphor has been that of a journey or a sea voyage. A leader, according to the analogy I suggested in the introduction, is like the captain or helmsman of a ship; leadership means navigating a course toward a destination, and motivating others to continue on that journey and labor toward its completion. In this chapter I switch metaphors—mid-stream,

---

1. From a meditation by Ken Untener (frequently attributed to Oscar Romero) in Untener, *The Practical Prophet*, frontispiece.

as it were—and invite us instead to view leaders not as helmsmen, ships' captains, or tour-guides, but as builders.

I do that for two main reasons. In the first place, the switch from viewing leaders as captains or helmsmen to viewing them as builders allows us to reflect on the plurality of leadership in a way that the helmsman metaphor struggles to accommodate.[2] The metaphor of *kybernēsis* implies a single, omnicompetent *kybernētēs*, who is expertly aware of "the time of the year, the seasons, the sky, the winds, the stars, and all that pertains to his art";[3] there is not really room for a committee at the helm.[4] When Paul speaks in 1 Cor 12:28 of *kybernēseis* in the plural (NRSV: "forms of leadership"), he is already putting strain on the metaphor, as does the use of the plural in LXX Prov 11:14; 24:6 to refer to "an abundance of counsellors." The metaphor of multiple architects, engineers and builders working together on a common project lends itself a little more readily to picturing that plurality.[5]

In the second place, the focus in this chapter on the metaphor of leaders as builders reflects the way in which the metaphor dominates Paul's language in 1 Cor 3, the section of 1 Corinthians on which we are concentrating in this chapter of the book. It is not the only metaphor within chapter 3 of the letter; within that chapter, Paul also evokes images of a leader as a breast-feeding mother of small children (verses 1–2) as a servant in a household (verse 5; cf. 4:1–2) and as a worker on a farm (verses 6–8). But it is the most prominent and developed metaphor, occupying much

---

2. Plato himself expresses a keen awareness of the limitations of his metaphor: "See how I strain after imagery. For so cruel is the condition of the better sort in relation to the state that there is no single thing like it in nature. But to find a likeness for it and a defence for them one must bring together many things in such a combination as painters mix when they portray goat-stags and similar creatures." *Republic* 488a.

3. Plato, *Republic* 488a.

4. Cf. Thomas Carlyle's famously authoritarian use of the metaphor to ridicule the idea of a ship attempting to round Cape Horn, steered by a democratic consensus; *Latter-Day Pamphlets*, 18–19.

5. The difference between the capacity of the two metaphors to picture plural leadership is only one of degree. On a large ship there are often multiple leaders with various spheres of expertise and responsibility, and even at the helm the job of steering must be done in shifts. Furthermore, on a large building project requiring teams of architects, engineers, and builders, collaboration is not necessarily easy or harmonious—coming to agreement about a common vision for the building and how to construct can, in some instances, be about as easy as steering a ship round Cape Horn by democratic consensus. But the fact that collaboration is necessary—whether or not it is easy—is precisely the point at issue in this chapter, and in Paul's use of the metaphor in 1 Cor 3.

of chapter 3 and spilling over into the language of the opening verses in chapter 4.[6]

The journey metaphor and the building metaphor are not incompatible. In particular, for the sake of our present purposes in this book, it is easy enough to find building-related equivalents for the dimensions of leadership that I have in earlier chapters pictured in terms of the destination of the journey and the direction and motivation required to reach it. A team working on a building project is no less a "purposive social system" than a ship's crew;[7] the project's completion corresponds more or less to the destination of the journey, the blueprints and specifications (and the problem-solving decisions that must be made along the way) provide a counterpart for the directive dimensions of the journey metaphor, and the motivation required to persevere and complete the building project is an obvious match for the motivation required to continue on the journey all the way to its end.[8] But the building metaphor provides an alternative way of viewing those dimensions of the task of leadership, and one that allows us to picture several other aspects of leadership alongside them. Within this chapter, then, the concept of leadership that we derived in the opening chapter from the journey metaphor will not be abandoned, but the metaphor itself will be put to one side temporarily, in favor of the image of the church as a construction project and leaders as builders.

---

6. See especially Bitner, "Constitution and Covenant," 227–334.

7. On "purposive social systems," see Hackman, "Leadership," 107.

8. All metaphors break down somewhere, of course. In the case of the building metaphor (and the farming one, for that matter) one point at which the metaphor breaks down is in its capacity to picture the continuities and connections between the particular ministries of leaders and overseers and the broader range of ministries in which every member of the community participates. In the building metaphor, the architects, engineers, and builders of the congregation may be plural (and the metaphor can be extended still further to include a multiplicity of laborers and sub-contractors) but at some point in the metaphor a line must be inevitably drawn between those who minister and those who are ministered to—"God's building," as Paul puts it in 1 Cor 3:9. It is difficult to picture oneself as simultaneously a brick and a builder. Another point at which the building metaphor breaks down (as Barth points out in CD 4/2:627) is in the way it struggles to accommodate the crucial element of *dis*continuity between the gradual progress of our present building work and the perfect completion of the building in the age to come. These two considerations are not reasons to abandon the metaphor, but they are points at which its limitations must be recognized, and it must be placed alongside other metaphors for church and ministry. Cf. Minear, *Images*, 221–49.

Corinthian Building

For Paul's original readers in first-century Corinth, the language and imagery of a building project would have been deeply familiar.[9] In the century or so since Corinth had been re-founded under Julius Caesar, the city had seen a vigorous and impressive series of such projects, and the boom had by no means come to an end in the time when Paul wrote his letter to the Corinthians; if anything, the surviving evidence suggests that building activity peaked during the time between Augustus and Nero.[10]

Building in Roman Corinth was not just a matter of pragmatic necessity; it was also an act of public benefaction and a vehicle for self-promotion. A revealing instance of this can be seen in a monument from first-century Corinth, the broken base of which survives to this day—a circle of stone columns standing on a square pedestal at the northwest corner of the Corinthian agora that bears (in giant carved letters, and not just once, but twice, in case you missed it the first time!) the inscription: "Gnaeus Babbius Philinus, aedile and pontifex, had this monument erected at his own expense, and he approved it in his capacity as duovir."[11] In the culture of ancient Corinth, those who had money were expected to spend it, not only on private buildings befitting their status, but also on public buildings that would serve some civic purpose and (at the same time) stand as monuments to their wealth and generosity.

The Corinthian Christians would not have been oblivious to this connection between building, benefaction and self-promotion; indeed the wealthiest members of the church may well have been in a position to participate themselves as benefactors in the civic life of Corinth.[12] Whatever

9. The metaphor of a community as a building would also have been familiar to Paul's readers through its frequent use in the language of Ancient Greek politics. (Cf. Mitchell, *Rhetoric of Reconciliation*, 99–111.) Paul's use of the metaphor here has some similarities to the standard political commonplaces, but is focused more on the status, agency and accountability of the *builders* than it is on the harmonious inter-relationship of the various parts of the building with one another. While the disunity of the Corinthian church is certainly in view within this chapter (cf. 3:4), Paul's more immediate focus is on the fleshly arrogance and adulation of human leaders that underlie the Corinthian factionalism.

10. Cf. Kent, *Corinth: The Inscriptions*, 23–26; Savage, *Strength through Weakness*, 35–36.

11. Cf. Kent, *Corinth: The Inscriptions*, 73; Murphy-O'Connor, *St Paul's Corinth*, 171.

12. Another surviving inscription from Roman Corinth, excavated in 1929, is the so-called "Erastus inscription," which reads: "Erastus, in return for his aedileship, laid this

Paul may have said about the rights and wrongs of their participation in this culture of visible public benefaction (and we should not assume that his attitude would have been entirely negative),[13] he was sharply critical of any assumption that ministry within the church, including ministries of leadership and benefaction, could be used similarly as a way of building monuments to the church's wisest and wealthiest.

Corinthian Christianity (3:1–4)

Yet that, it seems, was precisely the attitude that the Corithians were taking toward ministry and leadership, according to the opening verses of 1 Cor 3. Having laid out an account in 2:6–16 of the distinctively Christian wisdom that he calls "the mind of Christ," which is understood and received by "those who are spiritual," he turns to the Corinthians in 3:1–4 and laments how far removed from that their own thinking has been:

> And so, brothers and sisters, I could not speak to you as spiritual people, but rather as people of the flesh, as infants in Christ. I fed you with milk, not solid food, for you were not ready for solid food. Even now you are still not ready, for you are still of the flesh. For as long as there is jealousy and quarreling among you, are you not of the flesh, and behaving according to human inclinations? For when one says, "I belong to Paul," and another, "I belong to Apollos," are you not merely human?

For all their pretentions to superior wisdom and spirituality, the Corinthians are—in the very elitism that underlies their quarreling and jealousy—behaving precisely like the pagans of the city in which they live. Their behavior is "of the flesh . . . according to human inclinations . . . merely

---

pavement at his own expense." If the Erastus of the inscription was (as many commentators suggest) the same Erastus Paul refers to in Rom 16:23 as an *oikonomos* of Corinth, then he, for one, had his name carved (and inlaid in bronze!) into the stone of the city.

13. Cf. Paul's encouragement in Rom 13:3–4 to "do what is good" and receive the "approval" of the secular authorities, an encouragement that Bruce Winter takes as referring to the civic honors bestowed on generous benefactors; Winter, *Seek the Welfare of the City*, 25–40; 179–210. There is a subtle but important difference, it could be argued, between gratefully accepting honors bestowed in recognition of civic generosity and deliberately performing acts of ostentatious generosity in a quest for such honors. The Gentile Christian readers of the Luke's gospel—including people much like Paul's Corinthian friend Erastus—are forcefully reminded that the way of the Gentile rulers (who "lord it over" their subjects and are "called benefactors") must not be imitated among the followers of Jesus; Luke 22:25–26.

human"—that is to say, it mirrors the mentality and behavior that Paul has already depicted in chapters 1–2 as typical of the present age and those who wish to be counted great in it.

While "jealousy and quarreling" are the immediate symptoms that Paul names in verse 3, his response in the remaining verses of the chapter is not simply a reiteration of the importance of harmony and the evils of dissension; Paul goes deeper, to the disease that causes the symptoms, and offers a correction to the way in which the Corinthians are viewing leadership and ministry, and the proud, partisan boasting that goes with that viewpoint. To take up the building metaphor a few verses earlier than Paul does, it is as if the Corinthians view their leaders and teachers as builders of rival monuments, each one laboring on his own project, for his own glory, in order to win the admiration of his own followers and fans.

Building the Church (3:5–17)

Against that backdrop, Paul paints an alternative picture of how the work of leadership and ministry ought to be understood among the people of God.

Fellow-workers (3:5–9)

He begins with the leaders and ministers, and the way in which they are to be viewed in relation to each other and to God:

> What then is Apollos? What is Paul? Servants through whom you came to believe, as the Lord assigned to each. I planted, Apollos watered, but God gave the growth. So neither the one who plants nor the one who waters is anything, but only God who gives the growth. The one who plants and the one who waters have a common purpose, and each will receive wages according to the labor of each. For we are God's servants, working together; you are God's field, God's building.

The opening question—"What is Apollos? What is Paul"—receives a string of answers across the paragraph. Apollos and Paul are *servants* (verse 5)—not benefactors or masters, lording it over separate, personal projects of their own choosing, but laborers on tasks assigned to them by a common master. They are *farm-laborers* (verse 6), planting and watering the one crop, to which God is ultimately the one who gives the growth; hence, they are *nothing* (verse 7), apart from the one who causes the crops to grow. And they are *one* (verse 8; NRSV "have a common purpose")—not rivals or alternatives, but partners and collaborators.

Paul's analogy (drawn at this stage from the farm, not the building site) allows him to reframe the Corinthians' view of ministers and leaders in several important ways. It lowers their status from benefactors and patrons (with followers who say things like: "I belong to Paul . . . I belong to Apollos") to servants of a master; it acknowledges their diversity of roles ("I planted, Apollos watered") but insists on their unity of purpose; and it implies their interdependence on each other ("I planted, Apollos watered") while emphasizing their common dependence on God to grow their crops and reward their labor.

In summary, as Paul puts it in verse 9, drawing all these threads together: "we are God's servants, working together."[14] The parallel metaphors in the second half of the verse—"you are God's field, God's building"—reinforce the points Paul has been making in the preceding verses with a second set of mental images. Just as planting a crop is useless unless it is subsequently watered, and watering ground is pointless unless it has previously been sown with a crop, so laying a foundation achieves nothing unless it is subsequently built on, and building a structure is foolishness unless someone has first laid a foundation. And in both endeavors—the farm and the building site—the work of Christian leaders and ministers is pictured as the work of servants, laboring together on a common project, in a common cause, for a common master.

Paul's words here have an obvious and urgent relevance for those of us who serve in the churches of contemporary Western Christianity. There are subtle and important differences of context between the culture of patronage loyalties and honor contests into which Paul's letter was originally written and the culture of consumer capitalism in which we read it today, but Paul's argument still bites. The dynamics of the relationship between customer and brand, or between fan and celebrity, are somewhat more fluid than those that were typical in a patron-client relationship in the ancient world, and the quest for public honor was played out according to a different set of rules than the quest for market share with which we are more familiar. But those differences do not render Paul's words irrelevant—if

14. With the NRSV translators and commentators including Fee (*First Corinthians*, 134); Garland (*1 Corinthians*, 113); Thiselton (*First Corinthians*, 306); Ciampa and Rosner (*First Corinthians*, 149), I take Paul's expression here as meaning "fellow-workers (with each other) who belong to God," rather than "fellow-workers with God."

anything, the greater fickleness and flexibility of the modern context makes for more anxiety and competitiveness, not less, and amplifies rather than diminishes our need for the reframing that Paul accomplishes in these verses.[15] Whether we are ancients who have been conditioned to view leaders as rival citizens, questing against each other for the rewards of public recognition, or moderns who have been conditioned to view them as rival entrepreneurs, questing against each other for the rewards of business growth and market penetration, the analogy Paul offers in verse 8 is still apposite: the reward that matters is for the *labor* that leaders perform,[16] not for their talent, their wealth, their economic success or their publicly visible honor, and it is granted neither by the market nor by the city but by the Lord.

Careful work (3:10–15)

This calls for careful, dedicated, painstaking work, as Paul goes on to emphasize in verses 10–15, drawing out the building metaphor that he introduced at the end of verse 9:

> According to the grace of God given to me, like a skilled master builder I laid a foundation, and someone else is building on it. Each builder must choose with care how to build on it. For no one can lay any foundation other than the one that has been laid; that foundation is Jesus Christ. Now if anyone builds on the foundation with gold, silver, precious stones, wood, hay, straw—the work of each builder will become visible, for the Day will disclose it, because it will be revealed with fire, and the fire will test what sort of work each has done. If what has been built on the foundation survives, the builder will receive a reward. If the work is burned up, the builder will suffer loss; the builder will be saved, but only as through fire.

The care that Paul has in mind has at least two dimensions, pictured by the two ways in which he develops the metaphor. In the first place (verses 10–11), those who build must take care to remain grounded on the one foundation that has already been laid. In this sense, Paul's work as an *architektōn*—a master builder—is a metaphor for something more particular than just one

15. Cf. Wells, "The D-Min-ization of the Ministry," 177–78; Wells, *The Courage to be Protestant*, 25–39.

16. The Greek word used here (*kopos*) is a favorite Pauline word for the effort and toil involved in ministry (cf. 15:10, 58; 16:16), and fits well with the picture he is painting here of the hard, toilsome work done by slaves and farm-laborers.

kind of Christian ministry among a host of others. His role as apostle to the Gentiles—an authoritative, personally commissioned messenger of the risen Jesus—has been to lay the foundation on which all future building must take place. There is no call for religious geniuses to dream up new foundations for future wings and extensions to the building. And there is no need for the foundation—"Jesus Christ"—to be re-laid by later builders, who think that they have some better, deeper, more imaginative knowledge of Christ than that of his apostles. The one foundation of the church "has [already] been laid."

But there is more to the care that must be exercised than simply staying on the right foundation, making sure to color within the correct theological lines. Care must also be taken in "the sort of work" that is done on that foundation, pictured here by the metaphor of the building materials that are used. Just as the foundation-laying required the work of a "skilled" (*sophos*) master-builder, expertise and craftsmanship (in other words, wisdom) are also required of those who come after. As the metaphor suggests, and as I have already argued in a previous chapter,[17] this wisdom is a broad concept, embracing competence and creativity as well as correctness and character. Good building takes skill and practice. But the technical and experiential dimensions of that wisdom are not to be divorced from the distinctively Christian mindset and convictions that shape the way in which those skills and insights are to be evaluated and applied. Within the context of Paul's argument, the "wisdom" that is pictured in the metaphor of the skilled master builder should not be disconnected from the cross-shaped wisdom that he has already expounded at length in chapters 1–2. And the quality of the workmanship exercised by those who come after him must also be, by implication, an expression of the same wisdom. What counts as "gold, silver, precious stones,"[18] and what counts as "wood, hay, straw" will be judged not by worldly assessors but by "the Day." Much that is impressive to human eyes (including ministry that is built on the charismatic and rhetorical power of Christian leaders, or clever accommodations to the intellectual spirit of the age) is worthless in the sight of God and will not stand on the judgment day.

---

17. See chapter 4, above.

18. While most English versions translate *lithous timious* as "precious stones," conjuring up images of diamonds, rubies, etc., the more likely reference is to "costly stones" like marble and granite that are not only decorative but also substantial and durable. Cf. Thiselton, *First Corinthians*, 311–12.

Sacred work (3:16–17)

The care that must be taken in building God's church is further underlined in verses 16–17, where Paul further specifies the metaphor that he has in mind. The building in question, on which he and Apollos and all the various after-comers have been laboring, is not just any building but a temple: "Do you not know that you are God's temple and that God's Spirit dwells in you? If anyone destroys God's temple, God will destroy that person. For God's temple is holy, and you are that temple."

This means that the work done in building the church is sacred work, not only in the generic sense in which all work offered up to God is sacred, but also in an additional, more particular sense. It is sacred work because it is work directed toward the task of establishing and building up a community that is (uniquely and intimately) the dwelling place of God's Spirit. It is this conviction about the sacredness of the church as "God's temple" that underlies the fierceness of the warning Paul issues in verse 17 against those who act in such a way as to damage or destroy it. The warning here ("God will destroy that person") clearly goes beyond the picture that Paul paints in the previous paragraph of builders whose careless work ends up destroyed but who themselves end up "saved . . . as through fire." But the fact that it is immediately preceded and followed by a rhetorical question (verse 16) and a string of warnings (verses 18–23), which are clearly directed at the Corinthians, strongly suggests that the warning is still primarily intended for insiders, not outsiders. The kind of destructive activity Paul has in mind is that of vandals and saboteurs within the building side, not besieging armies outside the walls. Clearly, in Paul's mind, there is a way of behaving within the church (either as a leader, or as someone who "boasts" in the leadership of one against another) that is not just shoddy but destructive, and it will be rewarded at the last day with a terrible retribution.

Humble work (3:18—4:7)[19]

All of the various threads that we have traced in verses 5–17 converge in the string of warnings that Paul gives to the Corinthians in 3:18—4:7:

---

19. These paragraphs are also discussed in chapter 2, above, but without any reference to the way in which they relate to the building metaphor of 3:10–17, which is the focus of our discussion here.

Do not deceive yourselves. If you think that you are wise in this age, you should become fools so that you may become wise. For the wisdom of this world is foolishness with God. For it is written, "He catches the wise in their craftiness," and again, "The Lord knows the thoughts of the wise, that they are futile." So let no one boast about human leaders. For all things are yours, whether Paul or Apollos or Cephas or the world or life or death or the present or the future—all belong to you, and you belong to Christ, and Christ belongs to God. Think of us in this way, as servants of Christ and stewards of God's mysteries. Moreover, it is required of stewards that they be found trustworthy. But with me it is a very small thing that I should be judged by you or by any human court. I do not even judge myself. I am not aware of anything against myself, but I am not thereby acquitted. It is the Lord who judges me. Therefore do not pronounce judgment before the time, before the Lord comes, who will bring to light the things now hidden in darkness and will disclose the purposes of the heart. Then each one will receive commendation from God. I have applied all this to Apollos and myself for your benefit, brothers and sisters, so that you may learn through us the meaning of the saying, "Nothing beyond what is written," so that none of you will be puffed up in favor of one against another. For who sees anything different in you? What do you have that you did not receive? And if you received it, why do you boast as if it were not a gift?

The warnings that Paul urges upon the Corinthians in these verses are directed to the whole congregation, not exclusively to its leaders. Their special target is those within the congregation who "boast" in one leader against another, who are "puffed up," and who "see [something] different" in themselves that makes them distinguished and superior.[20]

But Paul teaches the general lesson about Christian humility by means of a more particular lesson about the humility of Christian *leadership*: "I have applied all this to Apollos and myself for your benefit, brothers and sisters, so that you may learn through us the meaning of the saying, 'Nothing beyond what is written,' so that none of you will be puffed up in favor of one against another." That is to say, the general point about humility has already been given particular, concrete form in the building and farming imagery of verses 5–17, as it was applied to the work of Christian leadership. Christian leadership models Christian humility by the way in which

---

20. Cf. the arguments in Fee, *First Corinthians*, 170–71, for reading the question in v. 7a this way.

it honors the work of fellow-laborers and refuses to compete with them for glory. It models humility by the way in which it respects the tradition in which it serves, consciously placing its work between those who came before and those who will come after, remembering not to indulge the fantasy that "my ministry" is my own private project, which I get to start and finish myself. It models humility in the way it labors carefully at its daily tasks of service, viewing its work more like the labors of a tradesman than the performances of a virtuoso or the compositions of a genius. Most of all, it models humility by the way in which it honors God, serving in fear and trembling before him, recalling that it is his assessment of the building work that counts above all else, and rejecting the delusion that it could improve on his plans and specifications by adding some flourish of its own that goes "beyond what is written."[21]

This means that the practices of Christian leadership, when they are performed faithfully, are humble, disciplined practices, in keeping with the humble, disciplined practices that make up the whole of the Christian life. This point is strikingly illustrated by Stanley Hauerwas in his chapter in *After Christendom* on "How we lay bricks and make disciples." The analogy is worth quoting at length:

> To learn to lay brick, it is not sufficient for you to be told how to do it; you must learn to mix the mortar, build scaffolds, joint, and so on. Moreover, it is not enough to be told how to hold a trowel, how to spread mortar, or how to frog the mortar. In order to lay brick you must hour after hour, day after day, lay brick . . .
>
> Of course, learning to lay brick involves learning not only myriad skills, but also a language that forms, and is formed by, those skills. Thus, for example, you have to become familiar with what a trowel is and how it is to be used, as well as mortar, which bricklayers usually call "mud." Thus "frogging mud" means

21. While the primary intended reference of "what is written" in 4:6 is most probably the Scriptures of the Old Testament (cf. Hays, *First Corinthians*, 68–69), it is possible to make a strong argument that the language of the building metaphors Paul has used in ch. 3 extends into the opening paragraph of ch. 4, and that the Scriptures (interpreted in the light of their fulfilment in Christ) are pictured here metaphorically as fulfilling the function of the contracts and specifications for the building project. Cf. Hanges, "1 Corinthians 4:6" for the argument that *ha gegraptai* refers to "some kind of document or legal contract" (188). While Hanges suggests that the particular document referred to here is likely to have been a set of written community by-laws, along the lines of the *leges sacrae* of the pagan cults, Bradley Bitner has pointed the way to another analogy, much close to hand, in the language of the surviving legal documents relating to Corinthian building contracts; cf. Bitner, "Constitution and Covenant," 227–334.

creating a trench in the mortar so that when the brick is placed in the mortar, a vacuum is created that almost makes the brick lay itself. Such language is not just incidental to becoming a bricklayer but is intrinsic to the practice. You cannot learn to lay brick without learning to talk "right." . . .

The language embodies the history of the craft of bricklaying. So when you learn to be a bricklayer you are not learning a craft *de novo* but rather being initiated into a history. For example, bricks have different names—klinkers, etc.—to denote different qualities that make a difference about how one lays them. These differences are often discovered by apprentices being confronted with new challenges, making mistakes, and then being taught how to do the work by the more experienced . . .

All of this indicates that to lay brick you must be initiated into the craft of bricklaying by a master craftsman . . . The best teachers in a craft do not necessarily produce the best work, but they help us understand what kind of work is best. What is actually produced as best judgments or actions or objects within crafts are judged so because they stand in some determinative relation to what the craft is about.[22]

It is tempting to view the work of Christian leadership (and Christian ministry more broadly) through the lens of some other, more glamorous and socially elevated metaphor. The paradigm of a professional, for example, has an almost irresistible allure to it, and there are certainly some things that can be learned by comparing the work of a Christian minister with that of a doctor or a dentist or a lawyer. But there are still crucial dimensions of Christian leadership—how it is learned and practiced, and how it is to be esteemed and evaluated—that are more clearly perceived through the lens of the building-site metaphor which Paul provides us with here. Leaders are builders, working together on a vast and sacred project that began long before they first walked onto the site, and will continue long after they are gone; they learn the practices of their ministry—in part, at least—through respectful apprenticeship and patient, laborious repetition; and they answer not to the whims of the marketplace or the opinions of the powerful, but to the judgment of the master for whom they are building.

22. Hauerwas, *After Christendom*, 136.

Edification (8:1, 10; 10:23; 14:1–40)

The language of the building metaphor does not disappear from the text of 1 Corinthians at the end of chapter 3, or (for that matter) at the end of the first paragraph of chapter 4. It continues to be evoked throughout the rest of the letter, most obviously in the form of the verb "to edify" (Gk: *oikodomein*—literally, "to build"), which serves in the remainder of the letter as Paul's preferred word to describe the form that Christian love takes in its service of the church and the believers who belong to it. Leaders do not have a monopoly on edification; all of the members of the body are to "strive . . . for building up the church" (14:12). But our understanding of the goal and method of Christian leadership is still helpfully sharpened by placing it within this broader framework of ministry as edification.

Crucially, the language of edification (as Paul uses it in 1 Corinthians) serves as a reminder that the benefit that leaders offer to the individual belongs within the context of the "building up" of the whole community: "To edify is to build, to join stones and timbers into a strong house. What edifies the church builds the church . . . Whatever edifies the brother does far more than improve his moral behavior; it strengthens him in his position in this structured society."[23] Even when the "building up" in view is the destructive emboldening that Paul pictures in 1 Cor 8:10 ("if others see you, who possess knowledge, eating in the temple of an idol, might they not, since their conscience is weak, be encouraged [Gk: *oikodomēthēsetai*] to the point of eating food sacrificed to idols?") it is still pictured in terms of a person being cemented into a place within a social system—in this case, the idolatrous social system of the pagan temple.

At the same time as noting the communal context of Paul's edification language, we should not overlook the strong emphasis of 1 Cor 8 on the conscience of the individual fellow-believer and the equally strong emphasis of 1 Cor 14 on intelligible word-ministry as the principal vehicle for edification within the gathering. Paul does not have in mind the sort of communal formation that uses the power of ritual, discipline, and habituation ("thought control," to steal a line from Pink Floyd) as strategies for bypassing the intelligent, responsible rationality of the individual. Building up one's fellow-believers does not mean bullying them into compliance with the norms of the group or leaning on them to disregard the twinges of their conscience (8:3–12). And in the context of the gathering, according

23. Minear, *Images*, 164. See also Barth, *CD* 4/2:626–41.

to Paul's instructions in chapter 14, the kind of speech that builds up the church is speech that invites its hearers to "understand" (verse 2), "know" (verse 9), and "weigh what is said" (verse 29). This remains the case whether the speaking in question takes the form of instruction (verses 19, 31), revelation (verse 30), consolation (verse 3), reproof (verse 24), or an outpouring of praise or lament with which the hearers can join by adding their own "Amen" (verses 13–16). The individual is to be built up within the context of the community, but the community is not to be built up at the expense of the rational judgment and conscientious responsibility of the individual.

All of this, ultimately, derives from the nature and character of the God to whom both the individual believer and the community of the church belong. The God who is made known in the gospel is a God who draws close to the weak, giving his Son to die for them (8:11), incorporating them in his body (8:12), and embracing them in their weakness as a people known by him (8:3). And he is a God whose nature is "not of disorder but of peace" (14:33), whose people must therefore manifest in their common life a foretaste of the peace of his coming kingdom. But that kingdom has not come yet—at least, not in its fulness. The peace of the Christian community is not a static, comfortable peace, and Christian leadership involves something more than just the nurturing or policing of harmonious relationships among the church's members. The church, as we have already argued in previous chapters, is a pilgrim community *en route* toward a future destination, and a missionary community, with a common task to attend to. And it is to that dimension of the church's life, and the corresponding dimension of Christian leadership, that we return in the following chapter.

seven

MOTIVATION

1 CORINTHIANS 15:12–58

A leader is a dealer in hope.[1]

They sat them down upon the yellow sand,
Between the sun and moon upon the shore;
And sweet it was to dream of Fatherland,
Of child, and wife, and slave; but evermore
Most weary seem'd the sea, weary the oar,
Weary the wandering fields of barren foam.
Then some one said, "We will return no more;"
And all at once they sang, "Our island home
Is far beyond the wave; we will no longer roam."[2]

Inertia and Hope

Leadership, according to the definition I proposed in the opening chapter of this book, involves not only direction but also motivation. A leader serves a group not only by pointing a way forward and discerning a wise

---

1. Attributed to Napoleon Bonaparte; cf. Bertaut, *Napoleon in his own Words*, 52.
2. Tennyson, "The Lotos-Eaters," lines 37–45.

path to follow, but also by helping its members to persevere in following that path, motivating them to undertake and complete the journey.

If that is the case, then the deficiency that leadership seeks to remedy is not just the misdirection or aimlessness that does not know the right way forward, but also the inertia that lacks the will to follow it. That inertia can be the consequence of many causes—fear, for example, or weariness, or sloth—but the common enemy of all of these, and the chief engine of Christian perseverance, is hope.

There are, of course, other motivations that a leader may call on in summoning a group to keep on moving. Coercive force, for example, can work for a time, though a point can still be reached where demotivation is so profound that even the direst of threats lose their potency. The solidarity of a group too can be a motive for perseverance, but when the members of the group have lost their confidence in the reason for its existence or its prospects of fulfilling that purpose, such solidarity inevitably begins to fray. In any human endeavor, a common hope is a powerful motivating force, and in the journey of the Christian life it is central and irreplaceable among the motives for endurance.[3]

The special importance of hope among the motives for Christian perseverance does not only derive from the universal tendencies of human nature, or the shaping influence of a particular human culture. It also, and supremely, derives from the content of the gospel itself, which announces the conquest of death in the resurrection of Jesus. The hope that motivates and sustains a distinctively Christian perseverance is not just a generic optimism but "the hope promised by the gospel" (as Paul puts it in Col 1:23). And in 1 Cor 15, which most commentators agree to be the climax of the letter, it is to the gospel that Paul returns, in a lengthy and powerful appeal that concludes with his exhortation to them in the final verse: "Therefore, my beloved, be steadfast, immovable, always excelling in the work of the Lord, because you know that in the Lord your labor is not in vain."

---

3. Cf. the role that Christian hope plays elsewhere in Paul's letters, in such places as Rom 5:2–5; 12:12; 15:4; 2 Cor 3:12; Col 1:4–5, 23; 1 Thess 1:3; 5:8. While recognizing the crucial role played by hope in Paul's vision of the Christian life, we should not oversimplify the dynamics of the relationship between hope and the other dimensions of Christian existence. Rom 5:2–5, for example, is a striking reminder that the connection between the practices of Christian perseverance and the disposition of Christian hope is not a one-way street—it is "the hope of the glory of God" that enables us to boast in our sufferings, but it is at the same time (according to verses 3b–4) the experiences of suffering and the practices of patient endurance that God uses to strengthen character and sharpen hope.

Corinthian Inertia (1 Cor 15:32–34)

While Paul's exhortation is couched in the language of "steadfast[ness]" and "immovab[ility]"—on the surface, at least, the polar opposite of our own metaphor of movement toward a goal or destination—it is clear from the remainder of the verse that the kind of immovability he has in mind is not something passive or complacent. Rather, the stance that they are to maintain is one of energetic and persevering activity—"always excelling in the work of the Lord, because you know that in the Lord your labor is not in vain." Thus, while the language of the implied metaphor is closer to the building imagery we explored in the previous chapter than to the journey metaphor we have relied on for most of this book, Paul's rhetoric is still aimed at motivating the Corinthians toward an active, purposeful perseverance, stirring them out of a kind of communal inertia.

The best clues as to the nature and causes of the Corinthian inertia can be found in the middle of the chapter, in the rebuke of verses 32–34: "If the dead are not raised, 'Let us eat and drink, for tomorrow we die.' Do not be deceived: 'Bad company ruins good morals.' Come to a sober and right mind, and sin no more; for some people have no knowledge of God. I say this to your shame." If verse 32 stood on its own, it could be read as a depiction of an attitude only hypothetically relevant to the situation of the Corinthians—Paul could simply be saying: "If we granted the theology that some of you subscribe to, and denied the reality of a future, bodily resurrection, then the logical entailment of that theology would be the kind of lifestyle and attitude expressed in the saying, 'Let us eat and drink, for tomorrow we die.' But of course none of you think and act like that, so you should return to an understanding of the resurrection that is more coherent with the hope-filled, courageous pattern of your lives." But verse 32 does not stand alone, and the verses that follow do not suggest a reading of that sort. The implication of verses 33–34 is that the attitude and lifestyle expressed in the saying that Paul quotes in verse 32 have already taken root among the Corinthian Christians, eliciting the rebukes Paul feels compelled to administer.

The particular attitude and lifestyle Paul has in mind are dramatized in the saying that he quotes. For the letter's original recipients in Corinth, the saying would most likely have been heard with a double resonance. In the first place, read against the background of the Old Testament book of Isaiah from which the quotation is taken, it evokes a picture of the Jerusalemites whom the prophet is rebuking:

> You counted the houses of Jerusalem, and you broke down the houses to fortify the wall. You made a reservoir between the two walls for the water of the old pool. But you did not look to him who did it, or have regard for him who planned it long ago. In that day the Lord God of hosts called to weeping and mourning, to baldness and putting on sackcloth; but instead there was joy and festivity, killing oxen and slaughtering sheep, eating meat and drinking wine. "Let us eat and drink, for tomorrow we die." (Isa 22:10–13)

The picture evoked is of a city that has put its trust in a few pathetically inadequate military preparations, as if they were enough to keep the Assyrian armies at bay. In the make-believe world of their fantasies, it is a time for slaughtering sheep, not putting on sackcloth.

A second likely resonance of the saying for the Corinthians would have been an echo of the stereotypically Epicurean response to human mortality, as it was depicted in the caricatures of its critics.[4] Epicurus's attitude toward pleasure (which he viewed as the "first and kindred good" of humankind) was closely connected to his view on death; death, he insisted was not to be feared at all, since it was nothing but non-existence and (consequently) the end of all pleasure and pain. The way to be happily mortal, acccording to Epicurus, was "not by adding to life an unlimited time, but by taking away the yearning after immortality."[5] Whether the popular opinion was fair to Epicurus's original vision or not,[6] most people in Paul's day would have viewed the philosophy of Epicureanism as adding up to something pretty close to the view expressed in the saying Paul quotes from Isaiah: "Let us eat and drink, for tomorrow we die."

---

4. Plutarch, for example, disapprovingly quotes the Epicurean Metrodorus as asserting that the human calling is "not . . . to save the nation or get crowned by it for wisdom [but merely] to eat and drink wine, gratifying the belly without harming it." *Moralia* 1098C; cf. 1100D, and 1125D.

5. *Letter to Menoeceus* 127.

6. Epicurus himself was eager to repudiate the common caricatures of his view: "When we say . . . that pleasure is the end and aim, we do not mean the pleasures of the prodigal or the pleasures of sensuality, as we are understood to do by some through ignorance, prejudice, or willful misrepresentation. By pleasure we mean the absence of pain in the body and of trouble in the soul. It is not an unbroken succession of drinking-bouts and of merrymaking, not sexual love, not the enjoyment of the fish and other delicacies of a luxurious table, which produce a pleasant life; it is sober reasoning, searching out the grounds of every choice and avoidance, and banishing those beliefs through which the greatest disturbances take possession of the soul" (*Letter to Menoeceus* 131–32).

Taken together, these two parallel pictures of eighth-century Jerusale-mites and first-century Epicureans vividly dramatize what it means to say that "the dead are not raised." The Corinthians—or some, at least, among them—are maintaining a pattern of life that deals with the shadow of death by a kind of hedonistic denial, drowning any sober thoughts of future death and judgment in the pursuit of present pleasure and self-indulgence. For the wealthier members of the Corinthian congregation especially, surrounded by all the distractions of the comfortable present, the idea of a future, bodily resurrection must have seemed a distant and superfluous dream. To bor-row an image from another familiar story in the Greek tradition, they had become like the sailors of Odysseus's crew who had sat down among the lotus-eaters and joined them in gorging on the trees' honey-sweet, narcotic fruits, losing all memory of their home and all desire to travel on toward it.[7]

Amongst the various influences that would have encouraged this at-titude on the part of the Corinthian Christians, one particularly powerful one would have been the propaganda of the Roman Empire that empha-sized the *pax* and *salus* that had been achieved through the rule of Augus-tus and his successors. Buildings, coinage, inscriptions, rituals all inscribed a message along these lines into the daily experiences of Corinthian life. For those at the top of the social tree, who benefited most from the structures and systems of the Empire, this message would have been particularly at-tractive and believable.[8] But it was not imperial propaganda alone that fos-tered an attitude of this sort; pagan religious practice was overwhelmingly (though not exclusively) oriented toward the attainment of prosperity and safety in this present life,[9] and those who achieved those goals—those who "ate and drank" in abundance—were able, to some extent at least, to defer uncomfortable thoughts about the fact that "tomorrow we die." While 1 Corinthians scholarship of a previous generation made much of the "over-realized eschatology," which (it was argued) had taken root among the Co-rinthian believers as an interpretation of their experience of the Spirit, most recent commentators on the letter have agreed that there was no shortage of realized eschatology already on tap in the pagan culture of the city. To the extent that the Corinthians' experience of the Spirit contributed to their

---

7. *Odyssey* 9.91–97.

8. See especially the excursus on "Roman Imperial Eschatology," in Witherington III, *Conflict and Community*, 295–98.

9. Cf. Witherington III, "Salvation and Health," 146–50; MacMullen, *Paganism*, 53–57.

confidence that they were "already . . . rich; [already] . . . kings" (1 Cor 4:8), it was only building on a foundation that was already laid by the culture the Corinthians had grown up with.[10]

Those of us whose lives are surrounded by the wealth and hedonism of modern Western consumer capitalism will not find it difficult to see similarities between the Corinthians' situation and our own. We too "eat and drink" abundantly, and are immersed within an economy in which (over-) consumption is our primary function and a culture in which it is, for many, the primary source of meaning.[11] If there is a chronic weariness that we are susceptible to, it is not solely the product of our restless busyness, but also (for many of us) a consequence of our comfort and satiety. Meaningful, stable, enduring hope does not come easily when you're busy and bloated, fixated on your immediate comforts and pleasures, and preoccupied with the task of securing and extending them.[12] The challenges facing Christian leaders in our own time have much in common with those that Paul was confronting in his letter to the Corinthians.

UnCorinthian Hope (1 Cor 15:12–58)

If a problem of this sort is at the heart of the Corinthians' malaise, it helps to explain why Paul's response, here at the climax of the letter, is to give them not less eschatology but more.[13] The dominant note of 1 Cor 15 is that of Christian hope, grounded in the resurrection of Jesus as the promise of our own, and of the victory of God over every hostile power. Paul's way of motivating the Corinthians away from the comfortable inertia that he depicts in verses 32–34, and toward the persevering zeal that he urges in the closing verse of the chapter, is by renewing and undergirding their hope.

---

10. Cf. Ciampa and Rosner, *First Corinthians*, 4–5.

11. Cf. the classic account in Galbraith, *The Affluent Society*, 114–31.

12. Cf. Hamilton, *Affluenza*, 6–7; Stiegler, "The Disaffected Individual."

13. Cf. Ciampa and Rosner, *First Corinthians*, 180: "Corinthian problems are not to be attributed to their faulty theology or premature eschatology so much as to their conformity to the norms and values of pagan culture . . . [E]schatology is not so much the problem as it is the solution."

The Rhetoric of Hope

A careful reading of the chapter helps in teasing out the dimensions of the rhetoric that Paul employs toward that end.

Rebuke (15:33–34)

If we start in the middle of the chapter, with Paul's depiction of the Corinthians' attitude in verse 32, the most immediate and obvious dimension of the rhetoric with which Paul responds to it is a frontal assault of blunt and forceful rebuke. For Paul (according to the language he uses in verses 33–34), the attitude and lifestyle of those Christians who say by their words and their actions that "the dead are not raised" amount to a shameful imitation of "bad company"; a metaphorical drunkenness from which they need to sober up; a sinful pattern of speech and life from which they need urgently to turn aside; an evidence of a catastrophic defection from true knowledge of God. Thus, Paul does not shrink back from rebuking them directly, in the context of a letter that is to be read before the whole congregation, with the deliberate intent of evoking their shame.

Reminder (15:1–11)

But the shaming of verses 33–34 is not the first or the last word of the chapter, and Paul's summons to hope within the chapter involves much more than this verbal chastisement. The chapter begins not with rebuke but with reminder—not just a rhetorical "reminder" of what the Corinthians *ought* to know but a real reminder of what they *do* know. It is addressed to them as "brothers and sisters," implicitly affirming the genuineness of their faith in Christ, and directs their attention back to "the good news that I proclaimed to you, which you in turn received, in which also you stand, through which also you are being saved."

The fact that Paul is reminding his readers of something they already know does not mean that he views his reminder as merely a polite redundancy. This much becomes immediately apparent in the second half of verse 2: the gospel which the Corinthians have received, and in which they stand, is the message through which they are being saved "if" (and, by implication, only if) "you hold firmly to the message that I proclaimed to you—unless you have come to believe in vain." The reminder in these verses is clearly, in Paul's mind, an urgently necessary one. But it is still reminder of what the Corinthians already know and have already professed to believe, not a piece of new information or an argument aimed at persuading them to a new opinion.

The foundational role that reminder plays in the rhetoric of the chapter reflects both the centrality of the gospel to Christian hope and (as I have argued in chapter 5, above) the traditioned nature of the way in which the gospel functions within the church. If Christian leaders have the task of stirring up hope among God's people, the main way in which they are to perform that task is not by daily conjuring up new reasons for hope, but by daily reminding the church of the reason for hope which it has already been given. In this sense, Christian leadership points the church forward to where it is going by pointing it back to where it has come from. The example and argument and exhortation and rebuke that are also part of the work of Christian leadership are all grounded in the prior and unceasing task of reminding God's people of what they already know; those who fancy themselves capable of something cleverer or more visionary than that should find another calling.

Testimony (15:5–8, 15, 27, 45, 55)

The gospel message of which Paul reminds the Corinthians has at its core the testimony of the eyewitnesses to the resurrection of Jesus. The Corinthians are being reminded not of an idea or a moral maxim or an inspiring fiction, but of a series of historical truth-claims about the death, burial and resurrection of Jesus, asserted on the basis of the testimony of those who witnessed them: "that Christ died for our sins . . . that he was buried, and that he was raised on the third day . . . and that he appeared" (verses 3–5).[14]

The testimony of the eyewitnesses (Cephas, the twelve, the five hundred, James, the apostles, and Paul) is joined by Paul—deliberately and

---

14. Cf. Anthony Thiselton's brief comments on the implicit epistemology that underlies Paul's argument: "In philosophical terms we may therefore regard the resurrection of Christ as having, in Paul's view, a certain 'basicality' which should cause us to hesitate to discard what is known in theories of knowledge as a 'soft' or 'modest' foundationalism as against either 'strong' foundationalism (Descartes) or nonfoundationalism (postmodernity). Paul agrees that many Christian beliefs are *mutually* supportive, but gives a degree of primacy (*en prōtois . . . parelabon . . . kata tas graphas*, vv. 3–5) [to some particular beliefs within the system]." *First Corinthians*, 1218; emphasis original.

emphatically—with the testimony of Scripture.[15] The tradition handed on to Paul, and from Paul to the Corinthians, is not just that "Christ died," but that Christ died "for our sins in accordance with the scriptures." The same is said of his resurrection on the third day. Even in the very act of calling him "Christ," Paul is evoking the whole grand narrative of Scripture and its messianic eschatology. Throughout the remainder of the chapter (as is the case too in the rest of the letter) the testimony of Scripture is repeatedly heard, and is integral to Paul's interpretation of the significance of Christ's death and resurrection: "The last enemy to be destroyed is death. For 'God has put all things in subjection under his feet'" (verses 26–27); "If there is a physical body, there is also a spiritual body. Thus it is written, 'The first man, Adam, became a living being; the last Adam became a life-giving spirit'" (verses 44–45); "then the saying that is written will be fulfilled: 'Death has been swallowed up in victory.' 'Where, O death, is your victory? Where, O death, is your sting?'" (verses 54–55).

As one of the eyewitnesses whose testimony he catalogues in these verses, Paul is clearly—and crucially—doing something irreplaceable and unrepeatable within these paragraphs, which cannot be superseded or replicated by anything that subsequent Christian leaders say and do. But the language of tradition we have already observed in 1 Cor 15:1–11 suggests an obvious bridge between the role of Paul the eyewitness and the work of Christian leaders who follow after him. We ourselves are not the eyewitnesses, but the transmission of their testimony—and the testimony of the Old Testament Scriptures to which it was inseparably joined—is still at the very center of our work.

Example (15:7–10; 30–32)

The witness that Paul bears to the resurrection is not only in his words but also in the pattern of his life; what he passes on to the Corinthians is both an apostolic message that is to be believed and proclaimed, and an apostolic example that is to be imitated. Much of the time, of course, example is a kind of silent rhetoric; its contribution to the ethos of a speaker and the pathos of a speech is a matter of subtext, tacitly embedded in the shared

---

15. See especially Watson, *Paul and the Hermeneutics of Faith*, 16–17: "Scripture is not a secondary confirmation of a Christ-event entire and complete in itself; for scripture is not external to the Christ-event but is constitutive of it, the matrix within which it takes shape and comes to be what it is."

experience of speaker and audience, and does not need to find its way explicitly into the words that the speaker employs. But from time to time, for one reason or another, it does find its way to the surface of the text, as is the case (albeit fleetingly) at several points here in 1 Cor 15.[16]

The fact that Paul's own life-story is part of the testimony that he bears is already intimated in the opening paragraphs of the chapter, where Paul places himself as "last of all" among the witnesses of the risen Jesus (verse 8) and "the least of the apostles, unfit to be called an apostle" (verse 9), because of his previous life as a persecutor of the church. In the verses that follow, he offers a brief testimony to the transforming impact of the grace of God in his life, focusing on the hard work of his apostolic labors as proof that the grace of God was "not in . . . vain" in its effect within his life (anticipating the language and ideas of the exhortation he gives to the Corinthians in verse 58, at the close of the chapter). Here, as elsewhere (e.g., 1 Cor 16:15–16; Phil 3:19–30; 1 Thess 2:7–13; 2 Thess 3:7–13; Acts 20:34–35), it is the "hard work" of a leader that is highlighted, as evidence of the empowering presence of the risen Jesus, and as an example to be imitated by others.

But the example of Paul's life goes beyond merely the busyness of his labors. As the argument in the middle section of the chapter unfolds, Paul returns to his own example in verses 30–32, focusing this time not on the labors he engaged in but on the risks to which he exposed himself: "And why are we putting ourselves in danger every hour? I die every day! That is as certain, brothers and sisters, as my boasting of you—a boast that I make in Christ Jesus our Lord. If with merely human hopes I fought with wild animals at Ephesus, what would I have gained by it? If the dead are not raised, 'Let us eat and drink, for tomorrow we die.'" Here, the dangers involved in Paul's missionary activity serve a double function in his rhetoric. On the one hand, they add to the list of phenomena in the life of the Christian community that would be absurd and inexplicable "if the dead are not raised" (verse 29); on the other hand, they implictly cast shame on the self-indulgent comfortableness of those who merely "eat and drink,

---

16. The fleeting and elliptic nature of Paul's references to his labors and sufferings within this chapter (including the stubbornly opaque reference of verse 32 to his battle with "wild beasts" in Ephesus) suggests strongly that this is not new information for the Corinthians. Paul is not acting as his own publicity agent, seeking to persuade the Corinthians that he worked, took risks and endured sufferings—these things are already known to them. Rather, he is offering the Corinthians an interpretation of his labors and sufferings, and pointing to them as a datum within a larger argument about resurrection, and as an example for the Corinthians to follow.

for tomorrow we die." The Corinthians are to take them into account both at the level of their understanding, by embracing the doctrine of a future, bodily resurrection, and at the level of their behavior, by imitating the risk-taking and labor of the apostle in the conduct of their own lives.

Of course, hard work and risky behavior in and of themselves are not a sign of hope or a testimony to the resurrection of Jesus. Hard work, for example, may tell a story that has more to do with personal ambition, or greed for gain, or anxiety about the opinion of others. Risk-taking behavior can sometimes be an expression of the *absence* of hope, and the lack of a serious, long-term purpose. The witness of Paul's life carries the meaning that he attributes to it only when the work and risk are taken in the larger context of the story of his whole life, and—even then—only as that story is interpreted by the message of the death and resurrection of Jesus, whom Paul is imitating and serving, and on whom he has pinned his hopes. But his life-story, including his example of labors, risks and sufferings, is not a dispensable extra that can be neatly detached from the content of his message; the impact of the message of the resurrection in the life of the messenger is a demonstration that the grace of God at work in the message was "not in vain" (verse 10), just as the message, in turn, provides the assurance that it is "not in vain" (verse 58) that Paul and those who imitate him devote themselves in costly labors to the work of Christ.

Christian leadership that follows in Paul's footsteps and points to a hope that is solid and effectual must similarly be a matter of lived example, demonstrating the effect of that hope in the life of the leader. This raises some obvious questions about the way that leadership commonly functions in contemporary Western Christianity, particularly within the larger movements and institutions where it is almost impossible for the thousands of people who make up the group to have any meaningful, first-hand knowledge of the private worlds and daily lives of those who serve as their leaders. Given the economic and social structures of modernity, particularly in urban and suburban contexts, it is hard to imagine a set of social arrangements for contemporary Christian living that did not involve at least some large-scale movements and institutions of this sort; we would find it almost impossible, I suspect, to do without them, and there is something positively good about the blessings and efficiencies that they enable. But we should not imagine that the kind of distant, high-altitude, depersonalized modes of leadership that tend to be required at the pinnacles of such structures (the megachurches, the big seminaries, and the larger national and international parachurch organizations, for example) provide us with the template of what is ideal or normative in Christian leadership. If we make them the model that we idealize and imitate in all other contexts, then we risk emphasizing the grand, visionary, and strategic elements of leadership over the everyday, local, and exemplary. Somewhere within the structures and institutions of our common life we need room for leaders whom we can see and know up close, the pattern of whose lives we can scrutinize, evaluate, and imitate within a shared context of discipleship. We need people like Paul (and—still closer to home—like Timothy [1 Cor 4:17], Stephanas, Fortunatus, and Achaicus [1 Cor 16:15–18]) whose leadership includes the hope-driven, resurrection-empowered example of their lives.

Argument (15:12–19, 29–32, 35–44)

While the testimony of Scripture and of the witnesses to the resurrection serves as the foundation of Paul's appeal within 1 Cor 15, and the example of his labors, risks, and sufferings powerfully reinforces his own credibility as a witness and models the kind of response he is hoping for from the Corinthians, these are not the only rhetorical resources that Paul calls on to persuade the hearers of the letter. Much of the chapter is made up of rational argumentation, drawing inferences from already established premises, exposing logical incoherencies in the position of those whose opinion Paul is criticizing, and offering explanatory analogies to illustrate the inadequacy of his opponents' skeptical assumptions. As Anthony Thiselton points out, the form of Paul's argument in these paragraphs "underline[s] Paul's expectation that believing Christians will respect logical coherence and rational thought. He does not hesitate to appeal to it."[17]

Thus, in verses 12–19, Paul traces out a series of inconsistencies between what the Corinthian doubters say about the resurrection and what they believe about other things. If the dead are not raised, then a long series of logical consequences follow, as entailments of that position. He does something similar, too, in verses 29–32, pointing out the inconsistency between resurrection-skepticism and the practice of "those who are baptized on . . . behalf [of the dead]" (whatever that means!), and its inconsistency with the self-endangering practices of Paul and his fellow-missionaries. If the Corinthians are happy to approve of these practices,

---

17. Thiselton, *First Corinthians*, 1217; emphasis his.

then it is inconsistent of them to reject the resurrection hope that explains and motivates them.

Another form of argument can be found in verses 35–44, where Paul enters into a brief, imagined conversation with a representative skeptic, whose scoffing questions he folds into the rhetoric of the chapter in verse 35: "But someone will ask, 'How are the dead raised? With what kind of body do they come?'" Paul responds with a string of analogies between the Christian hope of resurrection, built on the testimony of Scripture and the eyewitnesses, and various phenomena from the natural world that he considers to be part of the common knowledge of humanity. The point of the analogies is to expose the fallacious assumptions behind the skeptic's question, which assumes that the only kind of "bodily" resurrection Paul could have in mind would be one that merely perpetuated into the next life the same mortal, inglorious flesh that our bodies are made of in this life. Bodies—Paul counters—come in all sorts of different forms, with all sorts of differing kinds and degrees of glory; nature itself teaches this much, and Paul does not hesitate to appeal to the natural knowledge of his readers to support his rebuttal of the reductionistic materialism presupposed by his skeptical conversation partner.

The sheer quantity of argumentation that Paul includes within the rhetoric of this chapter, at the climax of the appeal that he is making by letter to his readers in Corinth, is an important reminder that the form of leadership Paul is modeling within the letter is one that does not bypass the intellect and understanding of his readers. His aim is not to dazzle or to browbeat or to coerce, but to convince, so that the zeal his letter stirs up is an enduring zeal, firmly grounded in the testimony of the gospel and a clear, coherent understanding of its entailments. The hope he seeks to foster is a hope that has its reasons.

Narrative (15:20–28, 51–57)

Talk about a concern for "rationality" and "logical coherence" within Paul's rhetoric in 1 Cor 15 should not imply that the overall schema within which Paul encourages his readers to make sense of their lives and the world they live in is a static, timeless system of eternal truths, laid bare in the treatises and theorems of philosophers and mathematicians. While Paul certainly has a place for assertions about God and the world that are permanently and universally true, the schema within which he urges his readers to make sense of their lives is not a static one, but is shot through with an irreducibly narrative dimension. Ben Witherington makes the point well:

> I have become convinced that all Paul's ideals, all his arguments, all his practical advice, all his social arrangements are ultimately grounded in story, a great deal of which is told in the Hebrew Scriptures . . . Paul's thought, including both theology and ethics, is grounded in a grand narrative and in a story that has continued to develop out of that narrative.[18]

Here in 1 Cor 15, the grand narrative that Paul sketches out for the Corinthians is explicit, sweeping, and triumphant. The resurrection of Jesus is narrated as the great turning point in a story that goes all the way back to Adam—his creation from the dust (verses 45–47) and his sin, in which "all died" (verses 21–22)—and stretches forward to consummation of all things, when all will be subjected under the feet of Christ, and Christ himself will hand over the kingdom to God the Father (verses 24–28). The exhortation to steadfastness, immovability and energetic labor in verse 58 is prepared for by a swelling narrative crescendo that promises and celebrates the hope of our own participation in Christ's victory, looking forward to the day when we will "bear the image of the man from heaven."[19]

The effect of this large, triumphant narrative is to evoke a joyful, bold, singing hope, that joins with Paul in taunting death (verse 55)[20] and giving thanks to God (verse 57). There is good reason why the strengthening and revival of the church has so often been accomplished by leaders who were, among other things, preachers and storytellers, who proclaimed to God's people the great narrative of his saving works and the promise of the things to come; and there is good reason too why the Scriptures are so full of songs like the songs of Miriam and Moses, Deborah and Barak, Hannah, David, Mary, and Simeon, that exult, sing, and triumph in the same story. If the

---

18. Witherington III, *Paul's Narrative Thought World*, 2; cf. Scott, *Paul's Way of Knowing*, 277–80.

19. Along with the NRSV translators, the UBS editors, and most modern commentators, I am following the manuscripts that read *phoresomen* ("we will bear . . .") not *phoresōmen* ("let us bear . . .") in verse 49; cf. the arguments in support of *phoresomen* as the more likely original, in Thiselton, *First Corinthians*, 1288–89; and Garland, *1 Corinthians*, 738. For the argument in favor of the contrary view, see Fee, *First Corinthians*, 794–795.

20. Paul transforms the summons of Death and Hades for judgement in Hos 13:14 into a taunt over death, whose penal role has been made redundant by Christ (cf. 1 Cor 15:56–57).

church is to be a people animated by hope, it will need leaders who tell and retell the great scriptural story of salvation history, and who so stir up the hearts of God's people that they lift up their voices in song.

Exhortation (15:58)

But the church is an army as well as a choir. The story that Paul narrates within this chapter is a big story; the hope that we ourselves will be raised and changed is embedded within a larger hope that "all things" (verses 27–28) will one day be under the feet of Christ. It is a battle story, that involves "enemies" (verses 24–26) who still oppose his rule. And it is, therefore, an unfinished story, whose consummation is still to come (verses 23–24). So Paul tells the story to evoke not only our joy and our singing but also our labor and our perseverance—or rather, our joyful, singing labor and perseverance. After the narrative of verses 51–57 comes the "therefore" and the exhortation of verse 58: "Therefore, my beloved, be steadfast, immovable, always excelling in the work of the Lord, because you know that in the Lord your labor is not in vain."

Whatever Paul has in mind as the precise content of what counts as "the work of the Lord" (and he shows no interest at this point in neatly defining it),[21] it is clearly something in which all of God's people are called to participate, something that makes no sense apart from the resurrection, and something that responds to the authority and call of the risen Jesus—it is "the work *of the Lord.*" Given the different situations and diverse gifts of the church's members, it will doubtless take many and varied forms. But it still derives its meaning and coherence from the name and story of the Lord Jesus, for whose sake it is performed. And Christian leaders are given the task of stirring up the resurrection-grounded hope that motivates God's people to keep staving off weariness and distraction, and give themselves wholeheartedly to it.

---

21. The activity that Paul has in mind when he refers to "the work of the Lord" and "your labor . . . in the Lord" is probably the shared task of building up of the people of God (cf. 3:10–15, 9:1) which is a task (unlike the futile labours to build something eternal on any other foundation) that withstands the predations of death and decay. The fact that Timothy is said in the following chapter to be "doing the work of the Lord just as I am" (16:10) does not require us to infer that it is the *exclusive* preserve of the apostles and their itinerant fellow-missionaries, or of those who are described in 9:14 as "get[ting] their living by the gospel."

eight

LOVE

1 CORINTHIANS 12:31 — 14:1

He who loves his dream of a community more than the Christian community itself becomes a destroyer of the latter, even though his personal intentions may be ever so honest and earnest and sacrificial . . . The man who fashions a visionary ideal of community demands that it be realized by God, by others, and by himself. He enters the community of Christians with his demands, sets up his own laws, and judges the brethren and God himself accordingly. He stands adamant, a living reproach to all others in the circle of the brethren. He acts as if he is the creator of the Christian community, as if his dream binds men together . . . When things do not go his way, he calls the effort a failure. When his ideal picture is destroyed, he sees the community going to smash. So he becomes, first an accuser of his brethren, then an accuser of God, and finally the despairing accuser of himself.[1]

The pursuit of excellence

A friend of mine recently lent me a book, written for Christian students and scholars, urging "excellence" (both moral and vocational) as an ideal to be pursued with diligence and zeal: "The God you serve is himself

---

1. Bonhoeffer, *Life Together*, 26–27.

characterized by excellence, and that same God has called you to the pursuit of excellence for his glory and for the good of others. If you pursue excellence and progress in it, you and others will be blessed, and God will be glorified."[2]

As I read his rousing summons to personal and professional excellence, I found my mind going back to my senior high school years and the time I spent at university, when the topic of excellence and its pursuit was very much present in my thinking, raising issues that exercised me enormously. When I was in my teenage years, the school I went to was devoted—*religiously* devoted, it seemed at times—to the quest for excellence. In almost every facet of school life, the message that was taught (or, at least, the message I absorbed) was that the meaning and purpose of the whole educational exercise was the measurable, competitive pursuit of excellence. "You may not be the best at everything," we were told, "but for each of you there will be something that you are particularly good at, some special gift or talent; your job is to find that thing—to be the best in the field and the best you can be."

For most of the way through high school I absorbed that creed and lived by it. I continued unthinkingly in that path until I got to almost the end of the final year of high school and started to ask myself what the point of all this pursuit of excellence was—what was the larger end that excellence itself was meant to serve. I started to become aware too of some of the arrogance in my heart, and of my tendency to classify and compare myself with others in order to boost my sense that I was someone, that I was good, that I was worth something.

By the time I finished high school and arrived at university I was becoming increasingly suspicious of the whole ideology of excellence and the decisions I had made that had been based on it. I had enrolled in a law degree, because that was what you did if your grades were good enough and you didn't want to study medicine. I stuck with that decision, at least to begin with, but I was dubious about the reasons why I had chosen it, and conscious of the need to have a better basis for determining what to do with my life. At times, I suspect, in the years that followed, I overcompensated by deliberately signing up for things that I wasn't so gifted at, ostensibly because there was a need there but also, at another level, as a way of repudiating the value-system that I had been surrounded by in my high-school years.

2. Köstenberger, *Excellence*, 232.

The questions I was wrestling with were personal and psychological ones, to do with how I perceived the expecations of my parents and the dependence that I felt upon external affirmation, but I suspect that I was not unique in my experience of wrestling with them. And they were spiritual and theological questions as much as they were psychological ones; among other things, they involved the theological problem of how to understand the relationship between gifts and love, which is right at the heart of the issues Paul addresses in 1 Cor 12–14.

Corinthian pursuits (14:12)

The Corinthians, in their own way, were no strangers to the idea of the pursuit of excellence. Paul talks about them, in chapter 14, as "eager for spiritual gifts"—more literally, "zealous for spirits." In context it seems that what he has in mind is their competitive quest for spiritual empowerments and abilities, as a facet of their larger quest for social esteem and advancement. They were a church that was deeply conscious of honor and appearance and reputation, and they approached issues of spiritual empowerment and ability within exactly that framework.

The most obvious gift that epitomized that attitude in the Corinthians was the gift of speaking in tongues; that was a really high-status gift in the Corinthian economy, and there was enormous kudos for those who possessed it. But there were other gifts and ministries that Paul includes in the discussion as well; among that wider list he talks about roles like those of apostles and prophets and teachers, and he also speaks more generally about "forms of leadership" (12:28). Clearly, in Paul's mind, the whole question of striving after spiritual empowerments and abilities that he is addressing in chapters 12–14 is closely connected with the issues of ministry and leadership. It's not only about healings and miracles and tongues.

Two cheers for giftedness (12:31, 14:1; cf. 1:4–7)

Paul does not throw a bucket of cold water over the whole idea. It's quite striking that in a communication to a church that was consumed with a competitive striving after gifts and a constant boasting in the possession of them Paul begins the whole letter with a prayer of thanksgiving to God for the gifts that the Corinthians possess: "I give thanks to my God always for you because of the grace of God that has been given you in Christ Jesus, for in every way you have been enriched in him, in speech and knowledge of every kind—just as the testimony of Christ has been strengthened among you—so that you are not lacking in any spiritual gift as you wait for the revealing of our Lord Jesus Christ" (1 Cor 1:4–7).

Paul does not throw out the baby of gifts with the bathwater of boastfulness. It is unlikely that he is being sarcastic here, given the pattern of how he uses his thanksgiving prayers in his other letters, and how earnest he is about the sincerity of his prayer reports. He really does thank God for these gifts of speech and knowledge that the Corinthians have been abusing so badly. Pondering these opening paragraphs serves as a healthy warning against the temptation to derogate giftedness and despise the whole discourse of leadership in reaction against the way they are so exalted and idolized within our culture. God-given ability and excellence and leadership are never to be boasted in or trusted as the bedrock of our hope; but they are to be received with thanksgiving and stewarded with wisdom. They are even, Paul says—along with all the other gifts God gives—to be pursued and striven for. So Paul says, in the verses that frame our passage in this chapter, "Strive [or "be zealous for"] for the greater gifts" (12:31); "strive for the spiritual gifts, and especially that you may prophesy" (14:1).

There are some commentators who argue that Paul could only have meant 12:31 descriptively and critically—"You are striving (wrongly, competitively, boastfully) for the greater gifts (and you shouldn't be)."[3] But that reading does not fit comfortably with what he goes on to say in 14:1. It really is, in both cases, an imperative, and one that is sincerely meant.[4] Paul's exhortation here (like his thanksgiving in 1:4–7) is extraordinary, when read within its context in a letter to a church whose members were already absolutely fixated on striving after gifts and excellences. Even when addressing a church like that of the Corinthians, there is something positive to be said about excellence and giftedness. It is a good thing to be zealous for gifts, including the gifts of leadership and teaching and wisdom and speech. If we serve as leaders among God's people, then we should not stop sharpening the tools God has given us; we should never cease from striving after excellence.

---

3. E.g., Martin, *The Spirit and the Congregation*, 34–35.

4. Cf. the discussion in Carson, *Showing the Spirit*, 53–58.

A still more excellent way

But there is something more excellent than excellence. That is to say, there is something more important—immeasurably more important—than simply being good, gifted, capable, outstanding at what you do. There is a greater end which all this excellence ought to serve. So Paul says, having given the first of his two cheers for giftedness in 12:31: "And now"—("And . . .", not "But . . ."!)—"I will show you a still more excellent way." That is the context of his famous poem about love in 1 Cor 13; it's framed on either side by exhortations about gifts and ministry and striving after greatness. And without sweeping those things aside, it throws a great arch over them and puts them stunningly, brilliantly, into a different context.

The indispensability of love (13:1–3)

In the first place (verses 1–3) Paul speaks about the indispensability of love: "If I speak in the tongues of mortals and of angels, but do not have love, I am a noisy gong or a clanging cymbal. And if I have prophetic powers, and understand all mysteries and all knowledge, and if I have all faith, so as to remove mountains, but do not have love, I am nothing. If I give away all my possessions, and if I hand over my body so that I may boast, but do not have love, I gain nothing."

Without love, all leadership and excellence and giftedness are nothing. Leaders are particularly prone to delusions of indispensability, and the phenomena that Paul singles out alongside the "tongues of mortals and of angels" as things that amount to nothing in love's absence—prophetic powers, understanding, mountain-removing faith, and grand gestures of benevolence and self-sacrifice—overlap significantly with the qualities that are celebrated and valorized in the cult of the heroic leader. The idolatry of leadership is not the only target in Paul's sights within this first stanza of the poem, but there can be little doubt that it is among them.

The character of love (13:4–7)

Then secondly (verses 4–7) Paul paints a picture of the character of love: "Love is patient; love is kind; love is not envious or boastful or arrogant or rude. It does not insist on its own way; it is not irritable or resentful; it does not rejoice in wrongdoing, but rejoices in the truth. It bears all things, believes all things, hopes all things, endures all things."

The list of qualities that Paul assembles in these verses intersects in all kinds of ways with issues of giftedness and ministry, but there are some very obvious ways in which it speaks quite specifically to leaders. Leadership involves a form of service that offers direction, that points to a particular path and says, "Let's go that way." But leadership exercised in love does not overlay that act of service with a self-seeking, self-affirming insistence on getting its own way; it doesn't allow the urgency of getting to that destination to be an excuse for impatience or unkindness; it doesn't lapse into irritability or resentment when its services are unappreciated or its efforts are frustrated. Whoever else these verses speak to, they certainly speak to leaders.

The permanence of love (13:8–13)

Then thirdly (verses 8–13) Paul speaks about the permanence—the eternal permanence—of love.

> Love never ends. But as for prophecies, they will come to an end; as for tongues, they will cease; as for knowledge, it will come to an end. For we know only in part, and we prophesy only in part; but when the complete comes, the partial will come to an end. When I was a child, I spoke like a child, I thought like a child, I reasoned like a child; when I became an adult, I put an end to childish ways. For now we see in a mirror, dimly, but then we will see face to face. Now I know only in part; then I will know fully, even as I have been fully known. And now faith, hope, and love abide, these three; and the greatest of these is love.

Love is not just a means to an end, a temporary necessity on the way to something else. Love is the end, both the journey and the destination, since God himself is love, from all eternity. One day God will be all in all, and human leadership will have served its purpose and reached its end. Leadership, with all the gifts and excellences that it deploys, has its part to play along the journey, but love is eternal.

Love and leadership

If that is the case, then love ought to be the last word of a book about leadership. Not all love takes the form of leadership, but all leadership—if it is to be *Christian* leadership—ought to be a form of love. Whatever your form of service, whomever it is you lead, whatever else you do, make sure that you love the people you lead. Loving an idea or a vision or an ambition is easy. Loving the church is hard. But it is what we are called to.

Love the whole global, universal church—even, or especially, if there are some points where you see faults and flaws in it, and ways it could be better. And love the local church to which you belong and in which you serve—not just your visionary dream of what the church ought to be but the actual, present church with all its imperfections.[5] Love the people whom you serve—patiently, kindly, generously, humbly, zealously, perseveringly; with warmth and devotion and loyalty and affection—and let your leadership be an expression of that love.

5. Cf. Bonhoeffer, *Life Together*, 26–27.

BIBLIOGRAPHY

Ancient and Patristic Sources

Alciphron. *Letters*. Translated by Allen Rogers Benner and Francis H. Forbes. In *The Letters of Alciphron, Aelian and Philostratus*, 38–341. LCL. Cambridge, MA: Harvard University Press, 1949.

Aristides. *The Complete Works*. Translated by Charles Allison Behr. Leiden: Brill, 1981.

Aristophanes. *Fragments*. Translated by Jeffrey Henderson. LCL. Cambridge, MA: Harvard University Press, 2007.

Athenaeus. *The Learned Banqueters*. 8 vols. Translated by S. Douglas Olson. LCL. Cambridge, MA: Harvard University Press, 2012.

Basil. *The Long Rules*. In *Ascetical Works*. Translated by Monica Wagner. FC. Washington, DC: Catholic University of America Press, 1962.

Dio Chrysostom. *Discourses*. In *Dio Chrysostom*. Translated by H. Lamar Crosby. 5 vols. LCL. Cambridge, MA: Harvard University Press, 1951.

Epicurus. *Letter to Menoeceus*. Translated by Robert Drew Hicks. In Diogenes Laertius, *Lives of Eminent Philosophers*, 2:648–59 LCL. Cambridge, MA: Harvard University Press, 1980.

Homer. *Odyssey*. 2 vols. Translated by A. T. Murray and George E. Dimock. LCL. Cambridge, MA: Harvard University Press, 1995.

Isocrates. *Orations*. In *Isocrates*. Translated by George Norlin. 3 vols. LCL. Cambridge, MA: Harvard University Press, 1968.

Origen. *Letter to Gregory*. In *The Ante-Nicene Fathers*, edited by Alexander Roberts and James Donaldson, 4:393–94. 1885. Repr., Peabody, MA: Hendrickson, 1994.

Plato. *Phaedrus*. Translated by Harold North Fowler. In *Euthyphro, Apology, Crito, Phaedo, Phaedrus*, 405–79. LCL. Cambridge, MA: Harvard University Press, 1914.

Plato. *The Republic*. 2 vols. Translated by Paul Shorey. LCL. Cambridge, MA: Harvard University Press, 1935.

Plutarch. *Moralia*. Translated by F. C. Babbitt et al. 16 vols. LCL. Cambridge, MA: Harvard University Press, 1927.

Plutarch. *Marcus Cato*. Translated by Bernadotte Perrin. In *Plutarch's Lives*, 2:302–85. LCL. Cambridge, MA: Harvard University Press, 1914.

Polybius. *The Histories*. 6 vols. Translated by W. R. Paton, Frank W. Walbank and Christian Habicht. LCL. Cambridge, MA: Harvard University Press, 2010–.

Strabo. *Geography*. 8 vols. Translated by H. J. Jones. LCL. Cambridge, MA: Harvard University Press, 1913–1927.

Modern Sources

Banks, Robert J., and Bernice M. Ledbetter. *Reviewing Leadership: A Christian Evaluation of Current Approaches*. Grand Rapids: Baker, 2004.

Barth, Karl. *Church Dogmatics*. Edited by G. W. Bromiley and Thomas F. Torrance. Translated by G. T. Thompson et al. 14 vols. Edinburgh: T. & T. Clark, 1936–1977.

———. *The Resurrection of the Dead*. Translated by Henry James Stenning. London: Hodder and Stoughton, 1933.

Bertaut, Jules. *Napoleon in His Own Words*. Translated by Herbert Edward Law and Charles Lincoln Rhodes. Chicago: McClurg, 1916.

Bitner, Bradley J. "Constitution and Covenant: Paul's Engagement with Roman Law in 1 Corinthians 1:1—4:6." PhD diss., Macquarie University, 2013.

Bonhoeffer, Dietrich. *Life Together*. New York: Harper, 1954.

Brookins, Timothy A. "The Wise Corinthians: Their Stoic Education and Outlook." *Journal of Theological Studies* 62 (2011) 51–76.

Carlyle, Thomas. *Latter-Day Pamphlets*. London: Chapman and Hall, 1850.

Carpenter, Christopher J. "Narcissism on Facebook: Self-Promotional and Anti-Social Behavior." *Personality and Individual Differences* 52 (2012) 482–86.

Carson, D. A. *The Cross and Christian Ministry: An Exposition of Passage from 1 Corinthians*. Grand Rapids: InterVarsity, 1993.

———. *Showing the Spirit: A Theological Exposition of 1 Corinthians 12–14*. Grand Rapids: Baker, 1987.

Cheung, Alex T. *Idol Food in Corinth: Jewish Background and Pauline Legacy*. JSNTSupp 176. Sheffield: Sheffield Academic, 1999.

Ciampa, Roy E., and Brian S. Rosner. *The First Letter to the Corinthians*. Pelican New Testament Commentaries. Grand Rapids: Eerdmans, 2010.

Clarke, Andrew. *Serve the Community of the Church: Christians as Leaders and Ministers*. Grand Rapids: Eerdmans, 2000.

DeSilva, David Arthur. *Honor, Patronage, Kinship & Purity: Unlocking New Testament Culture*. Downers Grove, IL: InterVarsity, 2000.

Fee, Gordon D. *The First Epistle to the Corinthians*. NICNT. Grand Rapids: Eerdmans, 1987.

Fotopoulos, John. *Food Offered to Idols in Roman Corinth: A Social-Rhetorical Reconsideration of 1 Corinthians 8:1—11:1*. WUZNT. Tübingen: Mohr/Siebeck, 2003.

Galbraith, John Kenneth. *The Affluent Society*. 40th anniversary ed. Boston: Houghton Mifflin, 1998.

Garland, David E. *1 Corinthians*. Baker Exegetical Commentary on the New Testament. Grand Rapids: Baker, 2003.

Hackman, J. Richard. "What Is This Thing Called Leadership?" In *Handbook of Leadership Theory and Practice*, edited by Nitin Nohria and Rakesh Khurana, 107–16. Boston: Harvard Business School Press, 2010.

Hamilton, Clive, and Richard Denniss. *Affluenza: When Too Much Is Never Enough*. Crows Nest, NSW: Allen & Unwin, 2005.

Hanges, James C. "1 Corinthians 4:6 and the Possibility of Written by-Laws in the Corinthian Church." *Journal of Biblial Literature* 117 (1998) 275–98.

Harris, Murray J., *Slave of Christ: A New Testament Metaphor for Total Devotion to Christ*. Downers Grove: InterVarsity, 2001.

Hauerwas, Stanley. *After Christendom? How the Church Is to Behave If Freedom, Justice, and a Christian Nation Are Bad Ideas.* Nashville: Abingdon, 1991.

———. *A Community of Character: Toward a Constructive Christian Social Ethic.* Notre Dame: University of Notre Dame Press, 1981.

Hays, Richard B. *The Conversion of the Imagination: Paul as Interpreter of Israel's Scripture.* Grand Rapids: Eerdmans, 2005.

———. *First Corinthians.* Interpretation. Louisville: Knox, 1997.

Jones, C. P. *The Roman World of Dio Chrysostom.* Cambridge, MA: Harvard University Press, 1978.

Kellerman, Barbara. *The End of Leadership.* New York: Harper, 2012.

———. *Leadership: Essential Selections on Authority, Power and Influence.* New York: McGraw-Hill, 2010.

Kemp, Rowan. "Sacrifice: Have We Given Up?" *Briefing* 382 (2010) 15–18.

Kent, John Harvey. *Corinth: The Inscriptions, 1926–1950.* Princeton: American School of Classical Studies at Athens, 1966.

Köstenberger, Andreas J. *Excellence: The Character of God and the Pursuit of Scholarly Virtue.* Wheaton, IL: Crossway, 2011.

Lendon, J. E. *Empire of Honour: The Art of Government in the Roman World.* Oxford: Oxford University Press, 1997.

Lightfoot, Joseph Barber. *Notes on Epistles of St Paul from Unpublished Commentaries.* London: Macmillan, 1895.

MacIntyre, Alasdair C. *After Virtue: A Study in Moral Theory.* 3rd ed. Notre Dame: University of Notre Dame Press, 2007.

MacMullen, Ramsay. *Paganism in the Roman Empire.* New Haven: Yale University Press, 1981.

———. *Roman Social Relations, 50 B.C. to A.D. 284.* New Haven: Yale University Press, 1974.

Martin, Ralph P. *The Spirit and the Congregation: Studies in 1 Corinthians 12–15.* Grand Rapids: Eerdmans, 1984.

Milbank, John, "Stale Expressions: The Management-Shaped Church." In *The Future of Love: Essays in Political Theology,* 264–78. Eugene, OR: Cascade, 2009.

Millikan, David. *Imperfect Company: Power and Control in an Australian Christian Cult.* Port Melbourne: Heinemann, 1991.

Minear, Paul Sevier. *Images of the Church in the New Testament.* 2nd ed. Louisville: Westminster John Knox, 2004.

Mitchell, Margaret Mary. *Paul and the Rhetoric of Reconciliation: An Exegetical Investigation of the Language and Composition of 1 Corinthians.* Tübingen: Mohr/Siebeck, 1991.

Mohler, R. Albert. *The Conviction to Lead: 25 Principles for Leadership That Matters.* Minneapolis: Bethany, 2012.

Murphy-O'Connor, J. *St. Paul's Corinth: Text and Archaeology.* 3rd ed. Collegeville, MN: Liturgical, 2002.

Oropeza, B. J. "Echoes of Isaiah in the Rhetoric of Paul: New Exodus, Wisdom and the Humility of the Cross in Utopian-Apocalyptic Expectations." In *The Intertexture of Apocalyptic Discourse,* edited by D. Watson, 87–112. Atlanta: Scholars, 2002.

Pickett, Raymond. *The Cross in Corinth: The Social Significance of the Death of Jesus.* JSNTSupp 143. Sheffield: Sheffield Academic, 1997.

Piper, John. *Desiring God: Meditations of a Christian Hedonist.* 4th ed. Colorado Springs: Multnomah, 2011.

Pogoloff, Stephen M. *Logos and Sophia: The Rhetorical Situation of 1 Corinthians*. Atlanta: Scholars, 1992.

Savage, Timothy B. *Power through Weakness: Paul's Understanding of the Christian Ministry in 2 Corinthians*. SNTSM. New York: Cambridge University Press, 1996.

Scott, Ian W. *Paul's Way of Knowing: Story, Experience and the Spirit*. Grand Rapids: Baker, 2008.

Smith, James K. A. *Desiring the Kingdom: Worship, Worldview, and Cultural Formation*. Vol. 1 of *Cultural Liturgies*. Grand Rapids: Baker, 2009.

Starling, David I. "The *Apistoi* of 2 Cor. 6:14: Beyond the Impasse." *Novum Testamentum* 55 (2012) 1–17.

Stevenson, Tyler Wigg. *Brand Jesus: Christianity in a Consumerist Age*. New York: Seabury, 2007.

Stiegler, Bernard. "The Disaffected Individual in the Process of Psychic and Collective Disindividuation." http://www.arsindustrialis.org/disaffected-individual-process-psychic-and-collective-disindividuation.

Sweet, Leonard I. *I Am a Follower: The Way, Truth, and Life of Following Jesus*. Nashville: Nelson, 2012.

Theissen, Gerd, and John H. Schütz. *The Social Setting of Pauline Christianity: Essays on Corinth*. Edinburgh: T. & T. Clark, 1982.

Thiselton, Anthony C. *The First Epistle to the Corinthians: A Commentary on the Greek Text*. Nigtc. Grand Rapids: Eerdmans, 2000.

Twenge, Jean M., and W. Keith Campbell. *The Narcissism Epidemic: Living in the Age of Entitlement*. New York: Free, 2009.

Untener, Ken. *The Practical Prophet: Pastoral Writings*. Mahwah, NJ: Paulist, 2007.

Watson, Francis. *Paul and the Hermeneutics of Faith*. London: T. & T. Clark, 2004.

Wells, David F. *The Courage to Be Protestant: Truth-Lovers, Marketers, and Emergents in the Postmodern World*. Grand Rapids: Eerdmans, 2008.

———. "The D-Min-Ization of the Ministry." In *No God but God: Breaking with the Idols of Our Age*, edited by Os Guinness and John Seel, 175–88. Chicago: Moody, 1992.

Windsor, Lionel. "The Perils of Plundering the Egyptians." http://matthiasmedia.com/briefing/2012/07/the-perils-of-plundering-the-egyptians/.

Winter, Bruce W. *After Paul Left Corinth: The Influence of Secular Ethics and Social Change*. Grand Rapids: Eerdmans, 2001.

———. "Culture's Challenge." *Australian Presbyterian* 607 (2008) 4–9.

———. *Philo and Paul among the Sophists: Alexandrian and Corinthian Responses to a Julio-Claudian Movement*. 2nd ed. Grand Rapids: Eerdmans, 2002.

———. *Seek the Welfare of the City: Christians as Benefactors and Citizens*. Grand Rapids: Eerdmans, 1994.

Witherington, Ben, III. *Conflict and Community in Corinth: A Socio-Rhetorical Commentary on 1 and 2 Corinthians*. Grand Rapids: Eerdmans, 1995.

———. *Paul's Narrative Thought World: The Tapestry of Tragedy and Triumph*. Louisville: Westminster John Knox, 1994.

———. "Salvation and Health in Christian Antiquity: The Soteriology of Luke-Acts in its First Century Setting." In *Witness to the Gospel: The Theology of Acts*, edited by I. Howard Marshall and David Peterson, 145–66. Grand Rapids: Eerdmans, 1998.

Wright, N. T. *The Resurrection of the Son of God*. Vol. 3 of *Christian Origins and the Question of God*. London: SPCK, 2003.

10411144R00075

Printed in Great Britain
by Amazon.co.uk, Ltd.,
Marston Gate.